County Council
Libraries, books and more . . .

2 3 NOV 2017

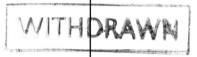
WITHDRAWN

Please return/renew this item by the last due date.
Library items may be renewed by phone on
030 33 33 1234 (24 hours) or via our website
www.cumbria.gov.uk/libraries

Cumbria Libraries
CLIC
Interactive Catalogue

Ask for a CLIC password

BRITAIN'S LOST CRICKET FESTIVALS

BRITAIN'S LOST CRICKET FESTIVALS

*THE IDYLLIC CLUB GROUNDS
THAT WILL NEVER AGAIN HOST
THE WORLD'S BEST PLAYERS*

CHRIS ARNOT

ACKNOWLEDGEMENTS

If I wore a hat, I'd raise it to the compilers of Cricket Archive, the website that has again proved indispensable for checking scores and performances on even the most obscure outgrounds from the day that they first hosted the first-class game. Many thanks as well to those who have shared their tales of summers past and taken the time to show me the sites of former grounds where so many cricketing memories are buried. Apologies to anyone inadvertently omitted from a lengthy list, in no particular order:

Matthew Engel, Stephen Chalke, Steve James, Harold Rhodes, Alan Oakman, Frank Hayes, Graeme Fowler, Mal Loye, Dennis Amiss, David Allen, Jack Russell, Alan Rayment, Peter Robinson, Colin Dredge, Stuart Turner, Ray East, David Banks, David Ward, Richard Gould, Bill Gordon, Bill Mustoe, Duncan Hamilton, Harry Pearson, Brian Halford, David Griffin, David Warner, Bill Kitson, Robert Whiteley, Peter Wynne-Thomas, Tim Jones, Norman Whiting, Derek Hince, Harry Patel, Ken Workman, Paul Biddlecombe, David Troughton, Peter Jouning, Rob Johnson, Steve Martin, Richard Holdridge, Mike Turner, Phil Aston, Martin Bowron, Robert Doleman, Roy Hillier, Mick Yates, Dave Allen, Brian Ford, Ken Maxsted, Peter Cockram, Bob Marsden, Pete Pritchard, Neil Probert, Jonathan Steeple, John Light, Roger Gibbons, Mike Askham, Maureen Coles, Jon Filby, Jay Webster, Clive Strickland, Chris Webber, Michael Davis, Diana Gibney, Baju Solanki, John Heiser, Martin Smith, Derek Creffield, Bill Pegram, Peter Dawson, Pat Kearney, Chris Deboss, Carol Boynton, Amanda Adegote, John Godden, Malcolm Bristow, Simon Beck, Brian Shackleton, Brian Mayers, Ray Hamer, Dick Brown, Mike Bruton, Dave Cresswell, Gerry Wolstenholme, Brian Johnson, Tim Wellock, Shaun Campbell and Doug Embleton.

Also thanks to Graham Coster for his advice and encouragement, to Robin Harvie and Melissa Smith at Aurum for bringing the book together and to Lucy Warburton for unearthing so many evocative photographs. Finally, a big thank you to my wife Jackie for her steadfast support, even though she's as enthusiastic about cricket as I am about *Strictly Come Dancing*.

IN MEMORY OF MY FATHER, RON ARNOT,
WHO INTRODUCED ME TO COUNTY CRICKET
AND BOUGHT ME MY FIRST BAT

First published in Great Britain
2014 by Aurum Press Ltd
74—77 White Lion Street
Islington
London N1 9PF
www.aurumpress.co.uk

A catalogue record for this book is available from the
British Library.

ISBN 978 1 78131 120 2

10 9 8 7 6 5 4 3 2 1
2018 2017 2016 2015 2014

Designed by Ghost
Printed in China

CONTENTS

'A thing of marquees where the right stuff could be found, and deckchairs and wooden chairs under which the spade and bucket could be parked for an hour or two.'

INTRODUCTION

~

The above quote is from the cricket writer R.C. Robertson-Glasgow who played for Somerset in the 1920s and 1930s. He was referring to Clarence Park, Weston-super-Mare, which, like the Recreation Ground, Bath, was essentially a public space that was transformed into a festival venue once a year. As Simon Hughes, another, more recent professional cricketer and writer, recalled, the pavilion was 'an enlarged park-keeper's hut, but barely adequate to keep chickens in'.

Everything had to be imported, including running water and electricity as well as seating and the beer tent. Not forgetting the toilets. Even at a venue as sedate as Dean Park, Bournemouth, where Hampshire twice won the County Championship, the whiff from the WCs could make the average bottom-of-the-garden privy seem positively fragrant.

But, then, cricket festivals were traditionally bucolic affairs. Part of our image of the game is of something timeless and vested in a traditional landscape. Timeless yet tied to the calendar. They gave a chronological rhythm to the cricket season. If it's late May or early June, Kent must be at Tunbridge Wells. August Bank Holiday? Time to head for Scarborough. (Two survivors there, but they're an increasing rarity, as we shall see.)

Festivals offered those who lived some distance from the county headquarters the chance to celebrate the sense of being a man (or woman) of Kent or Yorkshire, Lancashire or Sussex. They were intimate affairs that brought the players closer to the public than they would be at, say, Headingley or Old Trafford, or indeed any Test match arena where spectators wouldn't even be close to each other during county games. They also offered the chance to witness the world's greatest players in unlikely settings – the cricketing equivalent of seeing the Rolling Stones in a village hall or Wayne Rooney playing at the Crown Ground, Accrington. Wally Hammond smashed surrounding windows on his way to triple centuries at the Wagon Works Ground, Gloucester, and Rodney Parade, Newport. Sir Vivian Richards hit a six at the Town Ground in Worksop, Notts, that was heading for the boundary with Yorkshire before it collided with a cycle factory. His old pal and fellow knight Sir Ian Botham clouted one at Wellingborough School, Northants, that cleared the main road and landed in an industrial estate.

Botham and Richards, of course, belong to that most distant of periods, the day before yesterday. As, indeed, do the vast majority of cricket festivals. The lengthy list of lost outgrounds speaks for itself. There were sixty-four in 1961, an a profit in 2007, when the festival was a washout, because we insured against the loss.'

No chance of a washout in the glorious July of 2013. The Kent match, played under fierce sun and cloudless skies, was the first of two four-day games. Between and around them were three Twenty20 matches, two of which sold out all 5,000 tickets before a ball had been bowled.

As you may imagine, there were around half that number on the Friday that I attended. But there was still a buzz about the place at lunchtime, particularly in the large marquee put up by the Golden Heart Inn from the evocatively named Nettleton Bottom, Birdlip. Plenty of real ale in here, and you could have it in a proper pint glass rather than plastic.

Between savouring the Brakspear's and keeping an eye on the Trent Bridge Test, I talked about Folkestone and Maidstone with men of Kent as well as Leyton and Ilford with two blokes from Essex who were here simply here because they love coming to Cheltenham.

All four of those Kent and Essex outgrounds no longer host first-class cricket. The same goes for many more that you can read about, county by county, in the chapters that follow. With them has gone something special, something very English, something unique to each locality, I found myself reflecting in the soporific heat of early afternoon.

Even the batsmen out in the middle were briefly becalmed. All you could hear between occasional ripples of applause was the hum of the ice-cream van and, at one point, a distant siren as jarring as a fart in church.

No doubt it was far more raucous for those Twenty20 matches, but the crowds they attract are fundamental to the financial health of cricket. Those of us who prefer the four- and five-day versions of the game can't afford to be too precious about it. The same goes for sponsorship that would have seemed anathema in pre-war days when Saturdays at Cheltenham were the only annual holidays taken by Cotswold foresters such as John Light's father, a cousin of Laurie Lee's whose own father featured in 'The Uncles' chapter in *Cider with Rosie*.

Different times. Different values. Same game, more or less.

I hope that by dwelling on Cheltenham and Chesterfield I've conveyed a sense of just how pleasurable festivals can be. Most outgrounds harbour mere memories of those pleasures. Take away the buckets and spades and Robertson-Glasgow's view of Clarence Park, Weston, could apply to any number of former festivals that were once part of the 'loam and marrow' of an English summer.

▲ **Above:** *Sussex against Warwickshire at the picturesque Arundel Castle cricket ground in West Sussex.*

DERBYSHIRE

~

THE PARK, PARK ROAD, BUXTON

My train from Stockport is juddering alarmingly en route to the town with a cricket ground that was once the highest first-class venue in England. Buxton is over a thousand feet above sea level and the gradient has become steeper as the views become more spectacular. But this three-carriage 'chugger' seems to have the plucky staying power of Thomas the Tank Engine. We pull in bang on time. It's 12.51 on 28 May, nearly forty years on from the day that snow stopped play.

The match started on 31 May 1975, a hot Saturday. Blazing hot by Buxton standards. Supporters of Derbyshire and Lancashire, some of them stripped to the waist, were treated to an explosive opening day. The home side were 25 for 2 at the close, Lancashire having declared on 477 for 5. David 'Bumble' Lloyd had contributed 69, Frank Hayes 104 and Clive Lloyd 167 not out in as many minutes.

Revelling in comparatively short boundaries, the towering West Indies captain clobbered seven sixes to contribute all but eight runs to one of the fifty-partnerships that day. A game of bowls on the green next to the pavilion had to be abandoned for fear of flying leather. According to Derbyshire and England's Geoff Miller, 'it was as if an air-raid warning had gone off'.

Dickie Bird was umpiring and no doubt he'd 'never seen anything like it'. Not until the Monday anyway. Dickie would dine out for years on the story of what happened that day. He really hadn't seen anything like it. Nor had anybody else.

Derbyshire had recovered enough from the assaults of Saturday to defeat Glamorgan in a one-day game on the Sunday. Having had a rare summer's day off, Frank Hayes recalls that Monday morning driving 'over the top' from his home not far from Buxton along icy lanes bordered by white fields. What about the cricket field? 'It was covered by two inches of snow. I remember going out on it with Clive, David, Dickie and Peter Lever.'

Clive had never seen anything like it, coming from Guyana. Dickie had, coming from Barnsley – but not on the second day of 'flaming June'. He had no hesitation in calling off play for the day. So what did you do once the snowball fights had ceased, Frank?

'We liked a drink in those days so eventually we gathered round the bar and had a beer or two. There was no chance of playing again.'

Not on that Monday anyway. The unseasonal snow had settled thickly here in the High Peak. Only briefly had it interrupted a game between Essex and Kent at Colchester before melting away.

Summer reasserted itself on the Tuesday, a prelude to a heatwave. Dickie and his fellow umpire, Albert 'Dusty' Rhodes, felt able to allow the Derbyshire–

Lancashire match to recommence. Unfortunately, however, two inches of snow can wreak havoc on an uncovered wicket. Had three burly Buxtonians been called upon to pull the club's pre-war, formerly horse-drawn heavy roller, it may well have sunk.

Brian Bolus knew what to expect. After the first ball careered over his head, closely followed by a clod of earth, he turned to Farokh Engineer behind the stumps and muttered: 'Another fine nought then.' Perhaps the former Yorkshire, Notts and England player was being characteristically disparaging about his own batting. As it turned out, he made double figures in both innings, which is more than most of his team-mates did. Derbyshire were shot out for 42 and 87. It was their heaviest defeat of the twentieth century.

On his way out to bat, Ashley Harvey-Walker had removed his false teeth, wrapped them in a handkerchief and handed them to Dickie. 'He said not to worry because he wouldn't be in for long,' the venerable Bird told the *Daily Telegraph* in 2005. 'I'm glad to say he collected his teeth two overs later.'

In another, more recent interview with the *Buxton Advertiser*, Dickie summoned up more palatable memories of The Park: 'The food was excellent and they always made sure we had coffee and biscuits when we arrived. It was a very pleasant ground, set in beautiful countryside, and I think Derbyshire should return there to play a match.'

Which begs the question: why did they stop their long trek north in 1986, breaking a tradition that had begun in 1930 and continued every year, give or take a world war and a few problems with the wicket in the early eighties? While

▼ **Below**: *Derbyshire playing their regular Buxton fixture against Lancashire in June 1939.*

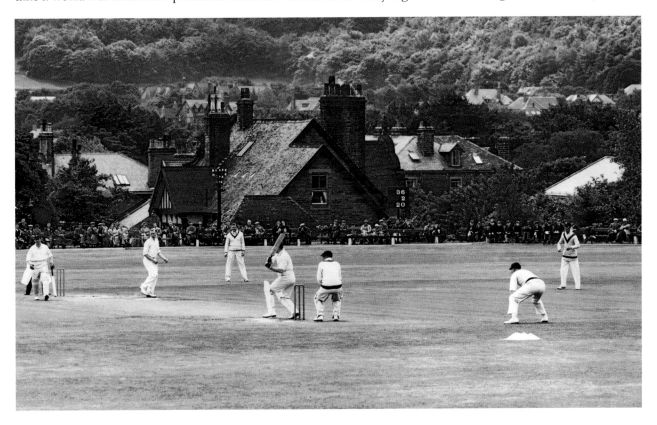

▼ **Below:** *Keeping hands warm on the way out to field – a sensible precaution on this ground.*

▼ **Bottom:** *Flatcaps and boaters much in evidence in the members' enclosure pre-war.*

▶ **Opposite:** *Michael Holding, who once clipped the pavilion roof at Buxton.*

the wicket and the weather may have been factors, it seems that the main reason was financial.

'Once Walter Goodyear [the groundsman at Derby] had come up and supervised the repairs to the wicket, we were granted a second-team fixture and then two more county matches,' says Peter Cockram, club trustee and Buxton first-XI captain for much of the sixties, seventies and early eighties. 'After that, Derbyshire started asking if we could get sponsorship.'

It must have been costing them a fair bit, I suggest. 'Well, we provided the ground and some fold-up seats from the Pavilion Gardens, but they also had to bring more temporary seating for between five and six hundred.' Bear in mind that driving from Derby to Buxton takes the best part of an hour, which meant that most home players would have to be found accommodation. Manchester is closer by around ten miles. That's why Lancashire provided the opposition for twenty-six of the forty-eight first-class games played here. 'At one time they would have been interested in taking it over as one

of their outgrounds,' Peter confides. 'The Lancashire committee of the 1950s used to love to come here.'

Certainly it would have made a pleasant change from the dark, satanic mills blighting Manchester's skyline at the time, I'm thinking, before he goes on: 'And some of the Surrey players who turned up here in the sixties used to sit outside the pavilion, take in the view and say that they wished they could play here every week.' Those were men, remember, who played home matches on a three-quarters empty Test ground dominated by a south London gasometer.

Even on a day like today, when rain rather than snow is lashing down, the Elysian Field beyond the pavilion window looks as though it might have been rolled out by the gods. Higher peaks than the one on which Buxton rests provide a dramatic backdrop. Mature trees encircle the foreground, partially obscuring elegant buildings in local stone. A mock-Tudor apartment block that sneaked in some time in the eighties can't quite spoil the setting. Cresting the ridge high above deep extra cover is what's known locally as Solomon's Temple, really a folly, built on the orders of one Solomon Mycock to provide work for the unemployed in the 1890s. And peeping over the foliage beyond a wide-ish long-on is the domed clock tower of the town hall.

It was there that Peter recalls going to seek sponsorship to keep the county coming. Alas, the High Peak Borough Council evidently felt that it had more pressing priorities. 'They said they couldn't find the money,' he shrugs. But didn't Derbyshire recently return to the Highfield ground in Leek for a forty-over match?

'They did. And that's because the Moorlands District Council chipped in £5,000. The chairman of that council just happens to be a cricket fanatic.' That's *Staffordshire* Moorlands District Council, since you ask. Like many another county, Derbyshire have never shied away from slipping over the border when it suits (see below).

Buxton is left with its memories. While playing for Derbyshire here in the eighties, Michael Holding launched a straight six that clipped the pavilion roof as it soared towards a high peak. Not even Clive Lloyd had belted one that far. 'Biggest hit I've ever seen

here,' Peter confirms. He also remembers the actor Trevor Howard having an all too brief encounter with the Park Road wicket while playing for one of the touring MCC XIs that used to take on Buxton every other year. He was out first ball.

Among the photographs on the pavilion wall is one of the county side in 1935. 'They went on to win the Championship the following year,' Peter points out. Just above them is another sepia-tinged shot of former full-time groundsman Percy Gander shaking hands with Buxton captain Bill Gillard in front of the old pavilion. It was taken in 1948 when Percy had not long arrived from Garrison A in Colchester, one of Essex's many outgrounds. He would stay at Buxton until the early sixties and one of his functions during county matches was to keep Les Jackson supplied with regular refreshment. Like Harold Larwood, another former miner, he felt the need for something stronger than orange juice to replace the sweat lost through giving his all with the ball. 'After twelve or fourteen overs, Les would slip off and Percy would have a couple of pints of Guinness

▲ **Above:** *The memorable day*
that snow stopped play.

waiting for him.'

Peter smiles at the memory and the grin grows wider as he recalls the first time that John Arlott arrived requiring something a little more refined than Guinness. By that time the John Player Sunday League was underway and coverage would be live on BBC2. Buxton's cricket 'festival' was really a three-day game interrupted by a forty-over match on what had previously been the Sabbath.

Arlott stopped off at the pavilion bar before heading for the commentary box at what was known as the 'bottom end'. His first enquiry went something like this: 'In this bar of yours do you have any good red wine?'

'I don't think we will have,' Peter hazarded.

'Why not?'

'We only drink beer up here.'

'Well, do you have any sherry or port?'

'Tell you what; I'll pop down to town for you. What would you like?'

And so it came to pass that the captain of Buxton first XI spent the opening overs of the ground's first John Player game truffling through the local branch of Victoria Wines in search of a decent claret. Arlott proved extremely grateful and paid up without demur. 'He was a character and a gent,' Peter reflects.

That would have been in July 1970, shortly after the Duke of Devonshire had opened the 'new' pavilion. Lancashire were again the opponents and a bumper crowd of well over five thousand turned out. They came up from Derby and Chesterfield and over from Manchester. The ground was so packed that some climbed trees to get a view of the game. Buxton had never seen anything like it.

That early June day when snow stopped play was still five years away.

IND COOPE GROUND, BURTON-ON-TRENT

From Buxton to Burton: different county and a very different setting. Same home team, though. Derbyshire travelled far and wide at one time, taking county cricket from the splendours of Queen's Park, Chesterfield (where they still play), to the former mining towns of D.H. Lawrence country, such as Ilkeston and Heanor. Between 1985 and 1990 they also played three one-day games at a place called Knypersley, which turns out to be in Staffordshire – as, indeed, is Burton.

The big British brewers that dominated the town before it became predominantly a haven for mass-produced lager could afford to pay full-time groundsmen to look after their cricket strips. Bass Worthington's low lying ground on the banks of the Trent hosted second XI county matches as well as two first-class games against the universities in the scorching summers of 1976 and 1977: Oxford one year, Cambridge the next. A promising youngster called Imran Khan hit 54 in Oxford's first innings and one Vic Marks, batting at number three, scored 98 in the second. Derbyshire still won by 81 runs.

But it was the ground owned by one of Bass's brewing rivals, Ind Coope, that won hands down when it came to attracting the county side from twelve miles down the road in Derby. The company's sports ground hosted thirty-eight first-class and seven Derbyshire List A games between 1938 and 1980.

Today it's the site of the Scientia Academy. A school, in other words. They were still building it when I called in and bumped into bowling-green groundsman Jack Tubey, a former Ind Coope plumber who used to supply water to the beer tents in the days when Derbyshire came to town back in the 1960s. Not to water the workers' beer, you understand, but to wash the glasses.

Today's health and safety precautions demand not only plastic glasses at cricket matches but hard hats when venturing within three hundred yards of a building site. 'You can borrow mine,' says Jack as I sneak off to take some pictures of the building rising rapidly over a cricket ground that was once a great source of local pride. Meanwhile, he carries on overseeing the cultivation of a new green to replace the one that will eventually become the school playing field. 'The kids'll be playing all sorts of games on there,' he says.

'Everything except cricket,' I suggest, and he nods before going on to bring up a memory of his own childhood – Les Jackson taking five wickets, including Don Kenyon's for a duck, as Worcestershire collapsed to 96 all out in their second innings to give Derbyshire what had seemed an unlikely three-wicket victory in 1953.

The Belvedere Bowling Club looks to be the only survivor from the sporting package offered by the Birmingham-based leisure company that owned this site the last time I was here in 2011. You could almost hear the sound of rheumatic knees bending in the sun as the crown-green bowlers went about their business.

My guide on that occasion was Pete Pritchard, chairman of Burton Cricket Club, and we were scouring muddy grass for evidence that our summer game had once been played here. 'I reckon this is where the pitch was,' Pete had ventured, starting on the goal line of one of several football pitches and pacing off towards the end where a substantial pavilion and clubhouse stood at long-off. 'You'd never believe it now, but you couldn't wish for a flatter, better wicket at one time.'

It could be a bit lively, however, back in the days of uncovered tracks. Nineteen wickets once fell in a day here in August 1958, when Derbyshire played Hampshire. Of that, more later. Pete stood twenty-two yards away across grass studded with the imprint of innumerable football boots. He was pointing one of his favourite Hamlet cigars towards the far corner of the Belvedere Road end where he used to sit in the scorer's box. 'It was an old wooden shed with a cord to pull the numbers round,' he recalled.

'The ground was heaving when Derbyshire came. And people used to look out of the upstairs windows of those houses,' he added, pointing his Hamlet towards a row of semi-detacheds beyond what was once the square-leg boundary. Other would-be spectators stood on the handlebars of their bikes and peered over the canvas sheet stretched along Belvedere Road in a failed attempt to keep out the prying eyes of those who hadn't paid.

Those in front of the pavilion, meanwhile, lounged in their deckchairs and savoured the occasion. 'There was always a good social scene, whether there was a club or county match here,' Pete told me. 'Spectators were sometimes joined by players in the bar after the match.'

By 2011 the Belvedere's clubhouse offered a range of locally concocted lagers and, mercifully, a solitary hand pump dispensing Marston's Pedigree. Ind Coope, which had become part of Allied Breweries in 1961, was later swallowed up by one of the multi-national brewing conglomerates that dominate the town today.

We were briefly joined at the bar by a crown-green bowler who sipped the froth from the first Pedigree of the day before taking his seat between two framed cricket bats. The one on the right was signed by and emblazoned with the image of Sir Richard Hadlee, formerly of Nottinghamshire and New Zealand, who apparently addressed a 'gentlemen's' sporting dinner here some years ago. The other, intriguingly, was signed by the West Indies team of 1928. Nobody seemed to know why. Not Pete, not the bitter-sipping bowler, nor his mate who had just

joined us in a sweatshirt with a Bass crest on the front.

What we can be more certain of is that Championship chasers Hampshire were here in the damp summer of 1958 and they did nothing to enhance their chances of landing a first title. Jackson and the then youthful Harold Rhodes ran amok on a drying pitch on 14 August.

The home side had lost one wicket for eight in the twenty-three minutes between showers on the

first day. As the sun came out that Thursday morning, they proceeded to lose their remaining nine for the addition of just 51. All out for 74 then, with Malcolm Heath taking 6 for 35. Farce was to follow as Hants were reduced to 23 all out. The visitors had enjoyed a tour of the brewery the night before, but it seems unlikely that overconsumption of Double Diamond had anything to do with their plight. Any team captained by Colin Ingleby-Mackenzie expected

long nights 'on the piss', but no batting side could have expected a long day on that pitch.

Harold remembers the visitors' skipper having a particularly bad time as the ball shot around. 'I'd hit him a few times – on the shoulder, the inside leg and the fingers more than once. Then he gloved another one that didn't carry. Colin was one of the bravest batsmen I've seen but, on that occasion, he cried out: "For God's sake somebody catch the bloody thing".'

Jackson finished with figures of 5 for 10 and Rhodes 4 for 12. Derbyshire went on to win an extremely low-scoring match after Hants managed 55 in the second innings. Ind Coope must have been a happy hunting ground for you, then, Harold? 'Yes, I got my cap there after that match and it seemed like a good place to play. The pavilion facilities were excellent with a proper balcony to look out from. The lunches were good and the hospitality could always be relied upon in the clubhouse lounge bar. We attracted good crowds as well. Wilfred Rhodes (no relation) lived in the area and my friend Graham Clarke used to give him a running commentary because he'd gone blind by then. Graham never had to say much, though. He told me that Wilfred had an extraordinary ability to tell what shot had been played by the sound of bat on ball.'

The great Yorkshire and England batsman would live on until 1973 when he was four years shy of his century. And Ind Coope? Cricket limped on there until five years into the new century, by which time the home team was Elvaston Castle third XI. Householders had long since ceased to peer out of their upstairs windows beyond the square-leg boundary.

◀ **Top left:** *The Ind Coope ground in in its festival heyday.*

◀ **Bottom left:** *The Bass ground that hosted two first-class games in 1976 and 1977.*

THE TOWN GROUND, HEANOR

There were at least three consecutive hot days in the summer of 1987 and, luckily, they coincided with Derbyshire's first match at Heanor. As far as the county was concerned, the town had one major advantage over Buxton. It was a damn sight closer to Derby. And, on the evidence of those three days in early July, it was damn sight warmer.

It was, however, nowhere near as attractive. Like nearby Ilkeston (see below) it lies in the Erewash Valley, which is – or was – mining country. 'The country of my heart,' D.H. Lawrence called it, although he couldn't wait to get away.

The Hampshire team that turned up to play

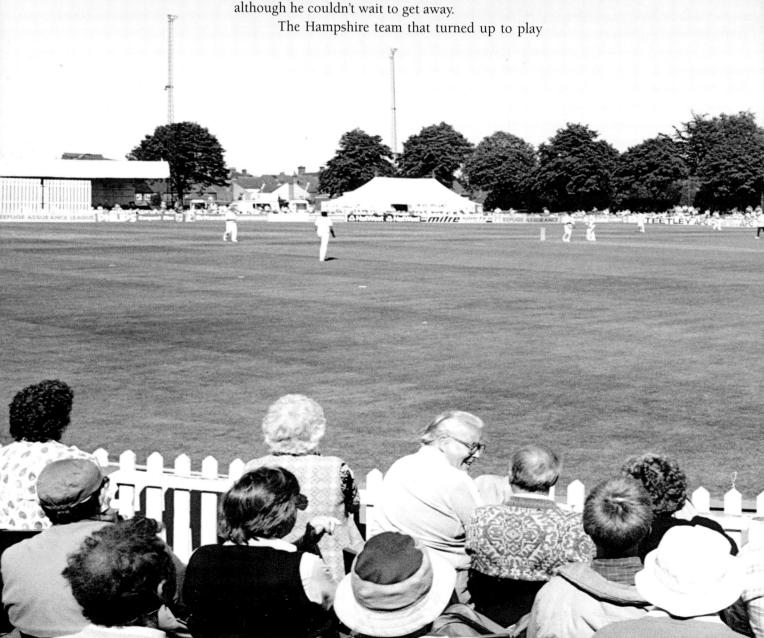

Derbyshire may well have felt the same, but their batsmen seemed to appreciate the wicket. Mark Nicholas and David Turner made hundreds as the visitors scored 349 for 2 declared and 261 for 6 declared. And they still lost with two balls to spare, Bruce Roberts hitting 106 and Kim Barnett falling just short on 91.

An exciting game, then, with plenty of runs. Well done, Heanor. Its reward was five more one-day games. No more first-class ones, however. The Town Ground was also the home of the local football club, which meant that there was the usual problem in these cases of part of the outfield being not quite as smooth as cricketers would like. So Heanor's first County Championship match was also its last.

The town Ground, Heanor,
enjoying its moment in the sun.

▲ **Above:** *Brian Close poses with his Somerset team before a match at Ilkeston.*

◀ **Left:** *Harold Larwood (left) and his partner in terror Bill Voce who scored 114 not out at Ilkeston in 1940.*

▶ **Opposite:** *Peter Denning batting for Derbyshire against Somerset at Ilkeston in 1977.*

RUTLAND RECREATION GROUND, ILKESTON

Even on a wet Friday lunchtime in the second decade of the present century, there's still a faded grandeur about the pavilion at Ilkeston. 'We're just fixing the guttering,' says one of the three groundstaff employed by Erewash Borough Council to maintain not only the slightly sloping but immaculately mowed cricket pitch but also bowling greens, tennis courts and more. With a golf club just down the road, there's also a sense of wide open green spaces here on the edge of a workaday former mining town, best known in south-east Derbyshire for the size and influence of its Co-op store.

Somewhere below the weathercock-topped clock on the pavilion frontage is the date: 1925. That just happened to be when Derbyshire paid their first visit for a county match. They carried on coming regularly, sometimes two or three times a season, until around 1980. Ilkeston staged proper cricket festivals and, compared to it, nearby Heanor was a johnny-come-lately and a one-match wonder – one first-class match anyway.

Ilkeston also hosted one-day games in the seventies, but county visits in both forms of cricket became increasingly infrequent during the eighties and nineties. The last was a four-day match in 1994 and the visitors were neighbouring Nottinghamshire, as they so often were.

Bill Voce, better known as Harold Larwood's partner in terror, scored 114 not out here for Notts in 1946. Six years later, Derbyshire put their neighbours to the sword, scoring 529 for 7 and winning by an innings. Cyril Poole must have been somewhat miffed about that, having posted 219 in the visitors' first innings.

Both games would have attracted large crowds in those post-war days. 'I'm told they used to sit in long rows all the way along there,' says the most senior member of the groundstaff, pointing to a row of wide steps, four or five high, on the left-hand side of the pavilion. But he doesn't know because, like his colleagues, he's too young to have witnessed the county coming to town.

It's time to get back to fixing that guttering.

DURHAM

THE RACECOURSE GROUND

A Geordie pal of mine shook his head in disbelief. His beloved Newcastle United hadn't won a trophy since lifting the long-forgotten Inter-Cities Fairs Cup in 1969. 'But look at Durham,' he beamed. 'They've just won the County Championship for the third time and Surrey have gone down. I never thought I'd see the day,' he added, shaking his head again. Like me, he was a child in the 1950s when Newcastle won the FA Cup three times, Surrey dominated domestic cricket and Durham were rarely talked about outside the North East.

They remained a minor county until 1991, which makes the new champions spring chickens in a game where the past is always present. Yet the weight of history hangs heavily down by the River Wear in the sylvan setting of the Racecourse Ground, home of Durham University Cricket Club and one of several outgrounds used by the county while its impressive stadium was being assembled by another riverside in Chester-le-Street.

The racecourse itself, laid out in 1733, has long gone. But it once attracted a crowd of 90,000 for a two-day event in 1873. The previous year saw the first Durham Miners' Gala gather on the same site. At its peak some 250,000 attended. It's an event that still goes on to this day, although there are hardly any working miners left, and it still draws sizeable crowds at the height of the cricket season.

'There's a fair bit of litter but no damage to the square, which is always fenced off,' I've just been told by former Lancashire and England opener Graeme Fowler who finished his career at Durham and went on to found a school of cricketing excellence at the university where he was once a student. He has also just reminded me of a poignant piece of cricketing history that happened here in July 1993.

A Durham side, new to the County Championship yet beefed up by imported players with more than a little experience, entertained the Australian tourists for what turned out to be Sir Ian Botham's last first-class game. It was twelve years on from his finest hour against another Australian side at Headingley and a sizeable crowd was further swelled by a large contingent of journalists and television crews.

'He must have been quite emotional at the end,' I suggest to 'Foxy' Fowler.

'No. He just walked off, sat down and said: "Well, that's that."'

There was a press conference later, needless to say, and the occasion rounded off many a television news bulletin that evening. But there was no appearance outside the pavilion for the crowds of paying cricket fans who had waited patiently outgrounds – pacy and bouncy enough to make Courtney Walsh virtually unplayable for the first few overs when Gloucestershire hiked their way up there in May 1994.

Wayne Larkins still managed to make 158 not out and Durham went on to win by 108 runs, yet that proved to be the last of Gateshead's five first-class games. Chairman Ian Rae claimed at the time that Durham's decision to pull out had left the club £12,000 out of pocket.

Goodbye Gateshead, then, but hello again, Hartlepool. Park Drive is a name that conjures up memories of nicotine-stained fingers and hacking coughs, but there's more than enough fresh air here at the leafier end of town and many remember the ground as being particularly attractive.

Northern Echo cricket correspondent Tim Wellock also remembers Durham winning both their matches there in 1994. 'John Morris made 186 as they beat Northamptonshire by an innings and an unbeaten 123 as they knocked off 262 against Glamorgan with three wickets to spare.'

But the favourite outground for his fellow members of the press, and indeed many Durham members, was Grangefield Road, Stockton – 'largely because of the hugely impressive efforts of the tea ladies'.

Despite Kent's Justin Kemp hitting a second-innings century there in 56 balls in 2007, a panel of umpires was brought in to deliberate on the state of the pitch. Why? Because the visitors had collapsed from 82 for 1 to 179 all out in their first innings.

One member apparently observed: 'If points are deducted because of the pitch, they should be put back on as a reward for the bacon butties.'

As it turned out, there was no deduction. But Durham, having joined the growing number of counties with Test-match status, never again returned to the more intimate and festive atmosphere of its outgrounds.

◀ **Left**: *Feethams in Darlington where football and cricket sometimes overlapped.*

ESSEX

∾

SOUTHCHURCH PARK, SOUTHEND-ON-SEA

R.C. Robertson-Glasgow must have enjoyed his trips to Southend with the pre-war Somerset sides: 'I miss the "profane multitude", the saunter from the hotel to the ground, punctuated by the vinegared whelk and relieved by the esculent cockle' he wrote. 'There were ducks on the cricket ground, which would quack the batsman with insolent prophecy to the wicket…' Or, as Jane Austen might have put it had she been around just after the Second World War: 'It is a truth universally acknowledged that a man reacquainting himself with the peaceful rhythms of an English summer after service overseas must have been in want of a county cricket match to watch.' The biggest draws on the circuit in 1948 were the Australian tourists.

There would have been a fair number of demob suits among the crowd of 16,000 that turned up at Southchurch Park in Southend on each of two days of the Whitsun Bank Holiday weekend. They were rewarded by seeing Essex become the first county to bowl out the Aussies that summer. In a day, what's more! There was just one problem: the visitors had accumulated 721 by the time stumps were drawn.

Keith Miller's contribution had been precisely nought. 'The story goes that he was playing cards and had a very good hand when a wicket fell after Bradman had put on 219 in ninety minutes with Bill Brown,' says John Heiser, a life member at Southend and a former member of the club's first XI. 'Miller turned to the other three in the card school and said: "I'll be back." He lifted his bat to the first ball from Trevor Bailey and was bowled. Bradman was furious apparently.'

Of the four centuries in the Australian side that day, the captain had top-scored with 187. John, thirteen at the time, remembers studying The Don's technique avidly while sprawled on his stomach, head cupped in hands, among the boys and youths thronging the grass around the boundary. 'I've seen a lot of top batsmen down here,' he muses, 'but Bradman was something else. His bat was light compared to the ones they use today and he was so wristy.'

Essex finally beat the Australians at Southchurch Park in 1964. Young John was pushing thirty by that time and there's a photograph on the pavilion wall of him laughing joyously among the crowd that gathered under the balcony as Trevor Bailey and his team took the accolades. 'Trevor was strutting up and down like Laurence Olivier milking a curtain call; that's why I was laughing. "I'm so overcome," he proclaimed.'

Nearly fifty years on and there's no balcony to stand on. The u-PVC windows

Southchurch Park, Southend.

through which we're gazing are all that's between us and the impressive spread of Southchurch Park's two cricket grounds: one used by Southend CC, the other by Old Southendians. The Southendians' pavilion is about two hundred yards to our right, beyond the edge of an expansive boating lake, and that was the one used by county sides and touring teams from 1906 until the early 1950s. 'They'd switched to this one when Lindsay Hassett brought the Aussies back in 1953,' John confirms.

Essex players saw the inside of many a far pavilion. Bear in mind that Chalkwell Park, just up the road in Westcliff-on-Sea (see below), also staged a festival until 1976, and the county also played sixty first-class matches at Vista Park, further round the coast in Clacton, between 1931 and 1966.

Players, officials and members were used to life on the road as they had no permanent home until Chelmsford began to establish itself as headquarters in 1967. Hardly surprising in the circumstances that Bailey called his autobiography *I've Been Everywhere, Man*. In it he lists nine different centres where he and his nomadic team-mates played 'home' fixtures, sometimes at more than one venue. Apart from the seaside resorts and Chelmsford, they appeared at

Brentwood, Colchester, Ilford, Leyton and Romford. Today only Lower Castle Park, Colchester, is granted a four-day and a one-day fixture.

The parting of the ways with Southchurch Park came shortly *after* Essex staged a four-day game against Notts and a one-dayer against Northants in 2004. By that time, the usual cost of setting up a festival had long been augmented by the consequences of persistent vandalism. 'Kids were getting into the park after dark and slashing the marquees with their knives,' says John, shaking his head sadly.

But that wasn't the end for Southend. Plans were drawn up for a regular festival at Garon Park at the far east of town, between a golf course and a huge sports centre that looks as though it recently dropped in from outer space. 'The ground offers a good atmosphere for a Pro-40 match and has the potential to expand to accommodate a crowd of up to ten thousand,' Southend CC secretary Baju Solanki assures me before going on to concede: 'It's not an ideal place to watch cricket when the weather's less than perfect.'

Essex committee members evidently had their doubts, too. In 2011 they voted to sever their first-team links. Baju hopes that they might still return one day for a Twenty20 match but, for the foreseeable future, that's

as close to a festival that Southend is going to get.

As for Southchurch Park, the white-painted, double-glazed pavilion that we're sitting in this morning is infinitely better appointed than the one with the rickety balcony that county players would recall. It seems that the local authority waited until after Essex had bid farewell before spending money on upgrading the changing room, showers and bar. By then, admittedly, the building was becoming something of a health and safety hazard. 'Graham Gooch came down here three years ago and his jaw dropped when he saw the new facilities,' John recalls.

'Goochie' had good cause to remember Southchurch Park with some affection. It was there, against Glamorgan in 1983, that he hit 176 in 117 balls, the highest score to date in a John Player Special League match. He also scored one-day centuries here on consecutive years in 1989, 1990 and 1991.

Ray East remembers beating Middlesex in two days of a first-class match here in 1968. 'It was an extraordinary pitch with the ball turning all over the place,' the former left-arm spinner says without mentioning that he made the most of it with figures of 5 for 33 in the first innings and 4 for 25 in the second. In the same June week, Essex lost by an innings to another Australian touring side. 'John Lever and me were trying to bat out for a draw,' Ray recalls, 'when John got hit on the pads. I could see it wasn't out, but the umpire Laurie Gray raised his finger anyway. "Sorry," he said, "I've got a train to catch."'

Ah well, at least Lever had lasted longer than Keith Miller twenty years earlier.

CHALKWELL PARK, WESTCLIFF-ON-SEA

The short boundaries at Chalkwell Park were always tempting for batsmen used to playing at larger county grounds. Having just arrived by bus from nearby Southend, I'm intrigued to learn that the Essex all-rounder Ray Smith once hit a six that travelled at least six miles on a double-decker. Luckily, there was nobody on the upper deck when the ball hurtled through the window. Maybe the conductor was a little on the deaf side. I'm reliably informed that the bus was halfway to Basildon before his attention was finally drawn to the smashed glass and the red-leather sphere under one of the seats.

Sixty years on and the only red-leather is out in the middle where three youthful members of the Westcliff-on-Sea Cricket Club are enjoying some early evening practice. There have been no county matches here since 1976 when Essex evidently decided that nearby Southchurch Park offered bigger boundaries and more space for spectators.

I'm struck by the fanciful notion that, apart from remaining a club cricket venue, Chalkwell Park also appears to have become an exercise space for greyhounds young and old. One has just shot past, only narrowly avoiding taking off my leg at the knee. Another has limped by on its own three remaining legs, enviously eyeing a mongrel peeing up a sapling.

Dutch elm disease has rather reduced the tree count in recent years, but

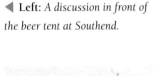

◀ **Left:** *A discussion in front of the beer tent at Southend.*

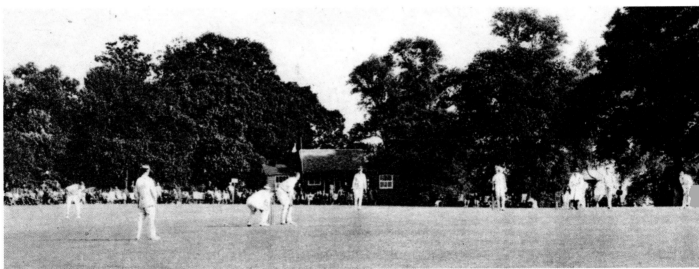

▲ **Above:** *Chalkwell Park, where the views were better than the loos.*

there's still a fine, spreading oak on the far side of the outfield and, after a damp day in east London, it feels good to be here under clear skies as the sun begins its descent towards its ancient boughs. Behind the pavilion is a fine view across the Thames Estuary, even if the horizon is dominated by the Isle of Grain Power Station.

Two boys are playing football on the forecourt of the pavilion which now houses a bar named after Trevor Bailey, a son of Westcliff, and proper flushing toilets, which should perhaps have been christened 'The Fred Trueman WCs'.

▼ **Below:** *Essex at Clacton in 1933. They beat Lancashire easily.*

'We'd tried for years to get planning permission to extend the building with loos and a bar,' says Derek Creffield, former chairman and first XI captain. 'But it was only after Fred told readers of the *Daily Telegraph* that Chalkwell Park offered the worst facilities that any professional player has had to put up with that the local council granted our wishes. We've been eternally grateful to Fred ever since.'

So where did players go to relieve themselves before Trueman's well-publicised grumble?

'If you wanted a sit-down job, you'd have to go to the public conveniences on the main road. Otherwise there was a lean-to with iron guttering at the back of the building and, believe me, it stunk to high heaven in hot weather.'

Apart from being a health hazard to pavilion users and passing bus passengers, Chalkwell Park at festival time could put the car dealer's premises on the other side of London Road under aerial assault. Windscreens on the forecourt were particularly vulnerable. Never more so than in July 1972, when Gloucestershire came to town with Mike Procter at the helm.

After scoring 51 in the first innings, he hit a brisk and blistering 102 in the second. The car dealer over the road would have been quite relieved when he brought himself on to bowl. Not so the Essex players who had to face those fearsome inswingers. They were bowled out for 137, with Procter taking 5 for 30, including a hat-trick of lbws.

Procter on that form could be unplayable and it wasn't just legs that got in the way of the ball. 'Poor old [Brian] Tonker Taylor was hit in the box,' recalls Stuart Turner, who must have been a little nervous. He was the next man in. 'What made it worse was that you could hear what was happening, but you couldn't see one of the ends from the pavilion at Westcliff. The side of a marquee was in the way.' What's more, the pitch was some way to the left. It was the one used by Leigh-on-Sea CC, who shared the same ground. Still do. Anyway, Stuart didn't have much time to sympathise with poor old Tonker. By the time the Essex captain and wicketkeeper hove into view after the long trek back to the Westcliff pavilion, he was on his way out to bat. Not for long, however. He was caught Swetman bowled Knight for 11. 'Only after one from Procter hit me on the elbow,' he remembers. 'To be fair, though, it wasn't a bad wicket.'

Not a bad setting either. With that spreading oak and those remaining healthy elms in full leaf, and the estuary beyond, it must have provided a fine vista at festival time. Just the sort of view, I should imagine, that you might appreciate from the top deck of any bus pulling up outside – just as long as you kept an eye out for flying leather.

VALENTINE'S PARK, ILFORD

A certain Mrs Ingleby laid down one condition when she granted Ilford Cricket Club a lease in 1897 on the parkland surrounding her stately home. The pavilion, she insisted, must be hidden away under the trees so that she didn't have to look at it. Were she able to see the current building, a squat, red-brick 1960s construction covered in garish advertisements, it might have brought on an attack of the vapours. But I must say that I'm more than happy to be invited inside by long-term member and part-time groundsman Chris Deboss as the drizzle that has been falling for much of the morning develops into a downpour.

Our subsequent conversation is conducted against the output of one of those radio stations that relays vintage comedy programmes. Quite appropriate in the circumstances because we're soon discussing the laughter that used to ring out through this room when the Essex team of the 1970s made their annual week-long sojourn for the Ilford cricket festival. 'Good lads they were,' smiles Chris fondly. 'Liked a beer and a butty.' Not necessarily at the same time. Before the start of play, there was usually a throng of players from both sides seeking

▼ **Below:** *The mobile scoreboard that followed the itinerant Essex team around.*

bacon butties made by Carol Boynton. She's here today, sitting at a table strewn with newspapers and tucking into a ham sandwich out of a packet.

Being a Muslim, Imran Khan gave the bacon a miss when he came here with the Sussex side, but then he had other things on his mind. 'He had to run away from all those Asian girls chasing him,' Carol beams between mouthfuls. Well, this is east London and the crowds here at festival time would have been increasingly cosmopolitan as the twentieth century advanced. Essex started visiting regularly in 1935 and called time just after the turn of the century in 2002. The county claimed that their visit was no longer financially viable – but that may have been because, at the request of Chelmsford members, the fixture had largely reverted to early summer when temperatures were lower and so were attendances.

Of all the Essex outgrounds, Stuart Turner reckons that Ilford had the best wicket. 'I made my maiden first-class century there in 1968,' he'd told me over the phone the previous day. 'Put on 192 with Robin Hobbs, and Hobbsy got a hundred as well. Mind you, the outfield was very up and down. If someone hit a ball at pace, you'd say to yourself, "Oh Gawd, I've got to get right behind this." You could easily make yourself look a fool. There were a

▼ **Below:** *Temporary turnstiles at Valentine's Park.*

▼ **Below:** *Trevor Bailey in characteristic pose.*

lot of West Ham supporters there for Sunday League games and we had a good rapport with them.'

Crowds of over seven thousand were not unheard of on sunny Sundays at Ilford in the 1970s and '80s. 'They'd be queuing four deep at the beer tent,' Chris recalls before pointing out a terraced area to right and left of the pavilion, now overgrown with grass and weeds. 'Those terraces would be covered with what we used to call "the rusties" – yellow seats with rusty legs supplied by some bloke with a lock-up in the Cambridgeshire Fens.'

By now Chris is in full reminiscence mood, recalling the Essex and England players, from Graham Gooch and John Lever to Nasser Hussain, who cut their cricketing teeth on this ground and tended to produce something special when they came back with the county side.

During the 1978 festival, Gooch hit 108 against Kent and then followed up by putting on a record second-wicket partnership of 321 with Ken McEwan against Northants. Lever took thirteen wickets in that match to follow up his spell of 4 for 6 against Kent. But even he must have been scratching his head four years later when Gooch, better known for his exploits with the bat, took 8 for 14 in eleven overs as Worcestershire were bowled out for 64. Following on, they were 17 for 1 when the rain came down and kept on coming all the following day.

Must have been a bit like today, I reflect, turning up my collar and splashing towards the bus stop after bidding farewell to Chris and Carol with another burst of canned laughter ringing in my ears.

▲ **Above:** *Smiling through the rain as Essex entertain the West Indians at Ilford 1957.*

▼ **Below:** *Essex v Lancashire at Ilford in June 1970.*

Sutcliffe and Holmes conrgratulated on their way back to the pavilion after a record partnership at Leyton in 1932.

The imposing pavilion at Leyton in its early heyday.

THE COUNTY GROUND, LEYTON

Leyton will always be cited by cricket historians as the venue where Herbert Sutcliffe and Percy Holmes put on 555 for Yorkshire's first wicket in 1932. It was a world record at the time and remains a record in England. The phrase 'as good as a Leyton wicket' – 'an idiom in cricketing language', according to the *Cricketer* magazine – had never seemed more apt. To mark the achievement there's a blue plaque on the side of the rather imposing half-timbered pavilion, built in 1886 at a time when this was the headquarters of Essex County Cricket Club. The County Ground remained just that until 1933 when Essex set off on their travels. They returned to Leyton in 1957 and continued to play two, sometimes three, matches a season here for the next twenty years.

Inside the pavilion is the 'Long Room': not quite as impressive as the one at Lord's, it must be said, but imbued with its own sense of history. There are some handsome sepia photographs on the walls, including one of J.W.H.T. Douglas, captain of Essex and England, who made his county debut here in 1901. The initials stand for John William Henry Tyler, although the Australians preferred 'Johnny Won't Hit Today', alluding to a somewhat cautious batting style that would have made Trevor Bailey seem like Viv Richards. In fact, Johnny could hit pretty hard without a cricket bat. He was also a useful middleweight who won a gold medal at the 1908 Olympics.

The Leyton Amateur Boxing Club occupies one of several buildings of more recent vintage that are beginning to make the pavilion look a little hemmed in. The ground lacks the sense of space that there is at Ilford where cricket is played in a public park, complete with flower beds and boating lake. It's difficult to believe that a crowd of 12,582 levered themselves into Leyton to see Essex play Worcestershire on August Bank Holiday, 1959.

These days the ground is used at weekends by the Asian teams in the National Cricket League – London's rather than Bangladesh's. The square, covered as it is in bad weather, is almost certainly better for batting today than it was in 1968 when Ray East remembers an extraordinary game against Warwickshire. 'I took fifteen wickets and we still managed to lose,' he says. In fact, he took 7 for 52 in the first innings and 8 for 63 in the second as the visitors managed just 98 and . . . er, 98. Essex was the only side to reach three figures – exactly 100 in their second innings. Alas, they managed only 47 in the first. So twenty-two players, each batting twice, managed to score 212 fewer runs than Sutcliffe and Holmes put on for their historic first-wicket stand.

By 1968, we must assume, the phrase 'as good as a Leyton wicket' would have seemed a little dated.

Above and below: *The scenes that greeted Sutcliffe's and Holmes' record*

THE OLD COUNTY GROUND, BRENTWOOD

An article in the 1969 edition of *Wisden* described the 'tree-surrounded acres of Brentwood' as forming 'one of the most beautiful of all the Essex grounds', before going on to maintain: 'To play at Brentwood is to feel that one is playing in the grounds of some vast country mansion.'

That may be so, but when Kent's Norman Graham was steaming in from one end there wasn't much time to admire the scenery. Ray East and Stuart Turner shudder at the memory of facing him there, also in 1969, when he took 8 for 20 and Essex were dismissed for 34. 'Brentwood may have been a beautiful ground, but it was a fearsome wicket,' Stuart recalls. 'Norman was a tall man in the mould of Joel Garner and he made it rear up from a length.'

Ray concurs. 'It was up round your ears when Norman was at you on that wicket, and there were no helmets in those days.'

Maybe the state of the wicket persuaded Essex to give the place a wide berth after the Worcestershire match of that year, bringing to an end a sequence of fifty-six first-class games that had begun in 1934.

Trevor Bailey looked on Brentwood as one of the most attractive grounds in the country, let alone the county. But then he also enjoyed his most spectacular spell of bowling there, taking 7 for 3 in 5.1 overs against Glamorgan. 'It was also the scene of my most stupid shout,' he wrote in *I've Been Everywhere, Man.* 'Against Somerset in 1951, the pitch was lively and slightly muddy, my field was ultra-attacking and I finished with seven wickets. In the course of my spell, somebody top-edged a hook which could have been comfortably caught by nine fielders and the keeper. While Doug Insole was deciding whose name to call, I shouted "mine" in a voice which brooked no interference and continued down the pitch. I finished full length and dirty about a yard past the stumps at the far end, while the ball landed safely another three feet further on and my colleagues dissolved into laughter.'

◀ **Left:** *Ashdown, Ames and Woolley in the days when Brentwood's wicket was perhaps not as fearsome as it would become.*

GLAMORGAN

AVENUE ROAD, ABERGAVENNY
(ONCE KNOWN AS PEN-Y-POUND)

Westward Ho!, then, and, as so often when I go west, the rain that began as a light drizzle has turned into a steady downpour by the time the train reaches Hereford. As we approach the border, I'm still hoping for the sort of meteorological miracle that sometimes happens in Wales when it can be raining heavily on one side of a mountain while the sun shines on the other.

Abergavenny's gorgeous ground, in the shadow of the Sugar Loaf, witnessed a miracle of kinds on the fourth day of a first-class match in late August 1997. While the rain lashed down all round, Avenue Road stayed dry enough for Glamorgan to chase down 197 to beat Northamptonshire. They went on to chase down the Championship at Taunton a week or two later.

Surprisingly for such a class batsman, Steve James hadn't previously made a significant county score at Abergavenny on what was considered a plumb batting wicket. But he made up for it during that match against Northants by scoring a century in each innings. 'It was the only time that happened in my career,' he tells me before going on to recall: 'I was going to the Arms Park to see Cardiff play Neath straight after the game and, as soon as we drove over the mountain, it was obvious that it had been bucketing down for a long time.'

Everywhere except Abergavenny, it seems. Steve already knew the ground well, having played club cricket there for his native Lydney. And he liked the place. (It would be difficult not to.) 'I enjoyed the intimacy of those outgrounds,' he says, recalling the walk through the pavilion bar on the way out to bat.

He also liked the food. 'Mention Abergavenny and I think first of the teas,' he wrote in the brochure brought out in 2009 to mark the club's 175th anniversary. 'Then of the lunches. Scrumptious. The way to a cricketer's heart is through his stomach.'

Take a bow, you women of the Willow Club, who not only produce meals of

quality as well as quantity. (Mike Gatting would have loved it had Middlesex ever ventured here.) The 'ladies', as they tend to be referred to in cricketing circles, have also raised much money for Abergavenny CC over the years.

What the local suffragettes would have made of that we can only speculate. They'd tried to burn down the pavilion, considered a male bastion, back in 1913. Unsuccessfully, it seems. But part of the building was badly damaged by fire in 1977, the year of the Willow Club's formation. Enough funds were raised by members of both sexes to rebuild and take the opportunity to extend the changing rooms and the catering facilities. Visiting county cricketers would have cause to be grateful for both.

Alas, the rain has not abated for my visit. So much for meteorological miracles. But even on a day like this the ground looks stunning. Low cloud is swirling around the ample girth of the Blorange Mountain away to our right as we look out from a spick and span pavilion bedecked with hanging baskets and bordered by troughs of well-watered flowers.

Asked what he thought of Avenue Road, Sir Vivian Richards drawled: 'It isn't exactly Lord's, man, but it's full of runs and the setting's good enough to be in the Caribbean.' That would have been in 1993 when Glamorgan beat Gloucestershire by 82 runs and Viv had been out in the nineties, as, indeed, was Matthew Maynard in both innings.

The few property owners hereabouts must have been relieved to see Richards striding back to the pavilion – particularly the owner of the house to our left where the boundary is on the short side and it's all too evident that quite a few tiles have had to be replaced.

Other top batsmen took full advantage of the close proximity of that boundary, including Graeme Hick, who features prominently among the centurions on the pavilion honours board. His top score was 252 for Worcestershire here in 1990 in a match that climaxed with Glamorgan chasing 495 to win, only to finish on 493 for 6.

Andrew Symonds went two better than Hick while playing for Gloucestershire in a four-day game at Abergavenny in 1995. In the process he scored sixteen sixes, a world record that was only equalled by Graham Napier of Essex in 2011, against

Surrey at Whitgift School, Croydon (see page 143).

Those tiles took a hell of a pounding from Symonds. 'Didn't the householder complain?' I ask Abergavenny CC chairman Brian Mayers.

'The ground was here first,' he shrugs. 'He never lets us have the balls back, mind. Not until the end of the season when a little pile appears on the boundary.'

Brian is one of several club stalwarts who gather here every Tuesday and Thursday morning to keep ground and pavilion up to scratch. Another is Ray Hamer, who has just driven me from the station. On the way he revealed: 'For county matches we used to hire cantilever stands. One of our main sponsors was a local building merchant and our secretary was one of the co-owners. So they let us have a stand free of charge. Arrived on a lorry, it did, and sort of cantilevered out.' At least it didn't fall off the back of a lorry.

That stand was sited across the ground from the pavilion and must have afforded a spectacular view of that flower-bedecked building with the Sugar Loaf Mountain behind it. All that's there now is what looks like a park bench. 'Old Codgers' Corner we call it,' says Ray. And it is on a corner, too – at the very point where the boundary rope seems to turn almost at right angles to accommodate a small bungalow with a garden that juts out. The local bowls club makes a similar intrusion on the other side, just to the right of the pavilion. Viewed from the top of the mountain, the ground would look a bit like a large, kidney-shaped swimming pool.

Glamorgan visited first for a couple of John Player League games in 1981 and 1982. They proved successful enough for the county to return for a Championship match the following year. And they continued coming until 1997. Yes, they pulled out after that exciting match against Northants on their way to landing the title.

Duncan Fletcher was the coach at the time and he apparently felt that the boundaries were too short while the journey for the home players, from Cardiff and Swansea over the Heads of the Valleys, was a bit too long. Then, surprise, surprise, there was the issue of money. Much had been spent on improvements at

Cardiff. Time to restrict the outgrounds to Swansea and Colwyn Bay, which had an abundance of holidaymakers and a generous grant from the local council.

Out of the blue, Glamorgan came back to Abergavenny in 2005, by which time Fletcher was otherwise engaged with England. Avenue Road was granted a game against the Bangladesh A team. 'Hell of a night that was,' Ray recalls. 'They came here, those kids – very disciplined, mind – and all the local restaurants put on a meal for them.' By that he means all the so-called 'Indian' restaurants which, like the majority of Indian restaurants in the UK, are run by Bangladeshis.

There's also a chain of chemists in the town run by the Shackleton family. Senior partner Brian Shackleton, after whom the pavilion bar is named, was chairman and is now president of Abergavenny CC. He has good cause to recall the last county match played there in 2007. Ten years after their withdrawal from Avenue Road, it seems, Glamorgan needed an extra outground while more work was done on what was, by that time, the Swalec Stadium. 'We were given the Leicestershire match and it was Paul Nixon's benefit year,' Brian recalls over the phone just before setting off on holiday. That was the good news. The bad news was that the match had to be abandoned without a ball being bowled. 'One day we hired a comedian to keep the sponsors happy and, luckily, they didn't ask for their money back.'

I don't need to spell out the cause of the abandonment. That's right: it rained solidly for four days. The people who run the most hospitable, eccentrically shaped and visually stunning ground used for first-class cricket in the UK could do nothing to stop it. Except pray for another meteorological miracle that never materialised.

▲ **Previous page:** *'It's full of runs and the setting's good enough to be in the Caribbean'* – Viv Richards on Abergavenny.

◀ **Opposite top:** *Cricket in the shadow of the Sugar Loaf at Abergavenny.*

◀ **Left:** *Colwyn Bay one of Glamorgan's two surviving outgrounds.*

THE GNOLL, NEATH, AND MARGAM STEELWORKS, PORT TALBOT

Glamorgan has had many an outground, some memorable, others all too easily forgotten. The county still holds festivals at Penrhyn Avenue, Colwyn Bay, and St Helen's in Swansea, which will live for ever in cricketing history. It was there in 1968 that Sir Garfield Sobers, or plain Gary as he was at the time, clouted poor old Malcolm Nash for six sixes in an over, a couple of which could all too easily have landed in the nearby sea.

And then there was the Margam ground in Port Talbot – 'an open, windswept field beside the steel works, a sulphurous smell of rotten eggs in the air and smoke billowing out of the chimneys,' as Stephen Chalke puts it in *The Way It Was*.

Nice setting, then. And the pitch? 'Spongy' was how *The Times* correspondent described it after a farcical game against Gloucestershire in 1962 when twenty wickets fell on the first day. Two years earlier Sussex had been the first county visitors and Les Lenham had managed to accumulate 51 in four hours. 'After every ball I had to go down the pitch and slam back down those great chunks of earth,' he recalled. 'It was an extraordinary place. You had to walk about seventy-five yards from the pavilion before you reached the boundary,'

Heaven knows what the Cambridge University side made of it when they arrived for the final first-class match in 1964. There were 17,500 employees at the steel works at the time and, on the third day, there wasn't one paying customer. The players came off for bad light for a while near the end of the match. 'There wasn't a cloud in the sky,' Glamorgan's Peter Walker told Chalke, 'but this orange smoke came

The Gnoll at Neath seemed like paradise compared to the Margum Steelworks' ground.

the Spa Ground when the opportunity arose seventy years after they'd departed for the Wagon Works.

Instead they headed for Archdeacon Meadow, and that's where we're heading now. We arrive around midday to find four fields full of children and youths playing matches in white flannels. It's an inspiring sight, albeit one tinged with regret on my part that such scenes are now a distant memory in schools outside the independent, fee-paying sector.

Gloucestershire played first-class matches, often with a one-day game as well, from 1993 to 2008, when problems arose with sponsorship and financial support from the County Council. Since then the county has returned only for Twenty20 fixtures, the last of which was in 2011. Anybody leaning on his bat at the end furthest from the red-brick pavilion would have a building that looks rather like an aircraft hangar behind him and a fine view of the cathedral, framed by two poplars, ahead. Henry Blofeld would also enjoy the frequency of double-deckers passing by to the fore and trains on the line to Bristol and South Wales to the left.

Whether Craig Spearman had time to take any of this in when he hit 341 here against Middlesex in 2004 is unrecorded. What we do know is that he hit forty fours and six sixes and that, despite scoring 383 and 358, the visitors still lost by ten wickets. Spearman's heroics surpassed Grace's 318 at Cheltenham and Hammond's 317 at the Wagon Works, yet, unlike them, he is a household name only in Gloucestershire and possibly his native New Zealand.

Talking of Hammond in 1936, celebrations of his triple century and Goddard's big pay day were followed by the grim news of the death in a motor accident of the county captain D.A.C. (Dallas Alexander Chancellor) Page on his way home. Only hours earlier he had taken the catch that had ended the match.

ERINOID PLASTICS, STROUD

It was known variously as the 'Turnip Patch' or 'Death Valley', by visiting batsmen at least. Bowlers looked on it with considerably more favour, particularly Gloucestershire's post-war spin quartet of Sam Cook, Bryan 'Bomber' Wells, John Mortimore and David Allen. It was David who once told me: 'The Erinoid festival was always at the end of May or the beginning of June and it was a good place to give your figures a boost before the Test selectors sat down.'

He duly delivered in the second match of Stroud cricket week 1963, with 4 for 59 in the first innings and 7 for 33 in the second as Glamorgan slumped to 76 all out. Gloucestershire won by ten wickets, just as they had against Leicestershire three days before. The Leicestershire team included one Dickie Bird who was

out for 7 in the first innings and was heard to mutter, as he trudged back to the pavilion: 'Eee, this is a hard way to earn a crust.' Arthur Milton managed to dip his bread in the same match, however, scoring 131 out of a Gloucestershire first-innings total of 336 – a very respectable score on such a pitch.

That Glamorgan game in 1963 was the last first-class match at the ground owned by Erinoid, manufacturers of buttons, umbrella handles, curtain rails and other plastic products. There had been fourteen since Nottinghamshire first came to call on a dampish opening day in 1956. Drizzle or downpours were not uncommon in the scenic valley in which the ground is set. 'A natural amphitheatre,' John Arlott called it.

Bomber Wells went into rather more detail while reminiscing for Stephen Chalke's book *Runs in the Memory*. He remembered the ground as 'long and

narrow, with this beautiful stream running down the side of it. Just an old wooden hut for changing quarters. All rough and ready, like the Stroud people, as good as gold. It didn't matter if you were Tom Graveney or old Jim Bloggs; they'd treat you all the same.'

Gloucestershire's current president John Light went as a schoolboy and continued to make the trip to Stroud as a student home from university. 'It was a crummy wicket, never really fit for county cricket, which was probably why we had to stop going there,' he recalls. 'But the festival was always a tremendous occasion.'

Certainly Bomber thought so. He remembered the dances put on in Erinoid's club room on Saturday nights. The local MP was there to greet the teams and, the food was 'absolutely superb' according to Bomber, who liked his tucker. Nobody danced, though. Not the Gloucestershire cricketers anyway. Captain George Emmett and senior pro Jack Crapp would have disapproved of anyone trying to trip the light fantastic. 'If you can get on a dance floor at the end of a day, you haven't been doing your whack in the middle' was the Crapp philosophy.

The ground now lies somewhere beneath the Bath Road Trading Estate on the edge of a housing estate of semis in reconstituted Cotswold stone. I remember being taken there by John Light and archivist Roger Gibbons when I was researching my book *Britain's Lost Cricket Grounds*.

Chuckles and chortles rolled around Roger's Peugeot 207 as more 'dear old' Bomber stories came out. Apologies if you've read this one before, but the day 'train stopped play' may be worth repeating.

One end of the ground here was known as the

Festival in full flow at Erinoid Plastics ground in Stroud.

railway end and a train driver in those pre-diesel, pre-Beeching days found himself a little ahead of schedule on the approach to Stroud station. So he stopped to watch the cricket for a while, seemingly unaware or unconcerned that steam was issuing from the funnel at a prodigious rate. Eventually the train moved on. The steam, however, stayed behind, leaving players and spectators in a thick fog for some time.

Our conversation in the car then turned to more serious matters as the Gloucestershire pair recalled one of the few visiting batsmen to master the track at Erinoid. Back in the early summer of 1959, M.J.K. Smith, also known as 'Mike', transformed the game after his Warwickshire side had been bowled out for just 115 in their first innings. According to team-mate Tom Cartwright, balls were shooting along the ground one minute and turning square the next. The visitors had expected to be packing their bags at the end of the second day.

▶ **Right:** *David Allen in his youthful prime.*

Enter MJK, horn-rimmed glasses aglint. 'I remember him sweeping Sam Cook into the river over there,' said John, shaking his head in disbelief. 'Nobody swept Sam like that. The crowd was stunned.' Smith went on to score 182 not out and guide Warwickshire to what had seemed a very unlikely four-wicket victory.

On the third day at Erinoid, it took a batsman with class to bring Death Valley back to life.

▼ **Below:** *Gloucester Cathedral looming over the pavilion at Archdeacon Meadow*

BATSFORD ROAD, MORETON-IN-MARSH

Richard Henshaw is something of a rarity in post-industrial Britain. He's a foundry owner. And what's more, a *Guardian*-reading foundry owner. It's his newspaper of choice in those rare moments when he's not overseeing the manufacture of brass castings or tending the square at his beloved Moreton-in-Marsh. ('Please don't call it Moreton-in-*the*-Marsh.') Finding a foundry in the Cotswolds in 2014 seems about as likely as your grandfather telling you that he once came across a teashop of honey-coloured stone in the Black Country of 1914.

Coincidentally, that was the year that Gloucestershire played their last first-class fixture on this ground. The outbreak of war was still three months away. W.G. Grace had finally hung up his bat eight years earlier and the only Foster in the Worcestershire side, M.K., hit 60 in the first innings of a low-scoring match won by the visitors.

Worcestershire would return quite a few times in the 1970s and 1980s for one-day games in the John Player League. So, too, would Warwickshire. After all, Moreton is in the north Cotswolds and the county boundaries are close by – a lot closer than the Gloucestershire county ground at Bristol. Other counties found their way from much further afield: from Kent, Sussex and Middlesex, for instance. 'Kent used to bring a surprising number of supporters with them,' Richard recalls. 'But then we've got a railway station just over three hundred yards away.'

How pleasant it must have been to stroll from the station along the Batsford Road, past the wooded area separating the boundary from a handsome recreation ground. It was into that copse that Alvin Kallicharan launched a spectacular six on his way to 101 in 1979. And sixes don't come easily on this ground. The boundaries are as far from the wicket as they would be at Bristol.

Entrance to the driveway at the side of Moreton-in-Marsh CC is through a five-bar gate with a sign pointing out that dogs are not allowed 'unless full members' and 'visiting teams are full members for the day'. To the left stands a lodge built in that honeyed Cotswold stone. Like the ground itself, it's

AT MORETON

UNTY TEAM,

◀ **Left:** *Gloucestershire players looking less than happy to be at Moreton-in-Marsh before World War One.*

◀ **Bottom left:** *Scoreboard and scorers' tent in the timeless setting of Batsford Road.*

part of Lord Dulverton's Batsford estate.

A line from *Macbeth* comes to mind on a midsummer's evening as 'light thickens and the crow makes wing to the rooky wood'. There's no shortage of birdlife round here. 'We had a parakeet take up residence once,' Richard recalls. 'The crows used to chase him out of those poplars beyond the sightscreen at the far end. He was only trying to be friendly,' he adds as a buzzard passes overhead en route to a mature oak tree that would have been getting on a bit even in the 1880s when Grace led out his Gloucestershire team on five occasions.

There were twenty-one List A matches played here altogether, from 1972 to 1996, attracting crowds of well over three thousand in some cases. Even those 'home' players who might have grumbled about the distance from Bristol, the size of the changing rooms, having to push their way through a throng of people in and around the pavilion to get to a wicket that was low and slow . . . even some of them might surely have felt inspired by the bucolic nature of the surroundings. Those with any soul might have felt the tug of their cricketing roots.

Admittedly, Courtney Walsh's roots were in Kingston, Jamaica, but he seems to have made a favourable impression on the locals in one of the more rural parts of his adopted county, despite that low, slow wicket. 'To see Courtney trying to get some bounce here was interesting,' Richard smiles. Did he become frustrated? 'No, he was great. Everybody loved him. He bowled tennis balls to my lad when he was about six or seven, running in fast then slowing down at the last minute to lob it up nice and gently. Oh yes, and Courtney always made a beeline for the burger tent where one of our local girls would give him one.' I beg your pardon? 'Give him a burger, I mean.'

Other tents offered tea, housed members and, in one case, showcased some of wicketkeeper Jack Russell's paintings. There was no beer tent, however. 'Everybody used the bar,' says John Curril, better known as 'JC', who tends the outfield. 'It was all hands to the pump on county matches. You'd be ready with the roller one minute and pulling pints the next. It used to get a bit congested in here and, as the day went on, one or two people weren't shy about voicing their opinions. I think some of the players felt that the public was a bit too close.

Did the players use the bar themselves?

Oh, yes. Quite a few would stay for a drink after the game. Norman Gifford liked it so much we almost had to push him out of the door. He was promising to come and play for us the following week.'

The bar harbours some comfortable looking chairs, including one or two high-backed Parker

Knolls of the sort that are advertised in the Weekend *Telegraph*. There are photographs all over the wall, as there are elsewhere in a pavilion built in the mid-sixties and largely financed through bingo sessions in the town hall. Look hard enough and you'll probably find more than one of Mike Procter who brought his 'Proctershire' side here for a benefit match in 1976. Presumably he scored some runs, I suggest. 'Of course,' Richard confirms. 'To see him hit a straight six on these long boundaries was quite a sight. At one point, so the rumour goes, he skied one to square leg and the umpire standing there said to one of our fielders: "I suggest you drop that one, young man." He duly did.'

The foundry owning groundsman has a more recent memory of being approached by an elderly man in fading health who had made a pilgrimage to Moreton-in-Marsh to see the wicket on which his great grandfather had dismissed WG while playing for Somerset. (That would have been one C.E. Winter, who trapped Grace lbw for 16 in 1885.) 'The poor man had travelled some way and he was dying of cancer,' Richard confides. 'He just sat down on the square.'

Perhaps we should never underestimate the tug of cricketing roots. Such is their depth that they go down to the Golden Age and beyond.

◀ **Left:** *The lodge building of Cotswold Stone where the window could be under threat from Mike Procter in full flow.*

HAMPSHIRE

DEAN PARK, BOURNEMOUTH

Just as Bogart and Bergman will always have Paris, so Hampshire supporters of a certain age will always have Bournemouth. Not only did Dean Park provide a beautiful backdrop for watching county cricket, it was also the venue where they won the County Championship. Twice.

The first time was in 1961 under the dashing captaincy of Colin Ingleby-Mackenzie. His team having seen off Derbyshire on the first day of September, a crowd gathered under the Dean Park pavilion balcony. They waited and waited and waited. And waited. When the Hampshire side finally appeared, the captain duly apologised for the delay and told them that he had been handing out the celebratory 'lemonades'.

Cue knowing laughter. This was a man who had once told a startled interviewer on a programme called *Junior Sportsview* that he attributed Hampshire's success to 'wine, women and song' and his insistence that his team should all be 'in bed in time for breakfast'.

The day after securing the title, they had to embark on another three-day

game. Yorkshire were regular visitors to Bournemouth's cricket week and their supporters booked their annual holidays accordingly. Jim Kilburn, the nearest thing to Neville Cardus east of the Pennines, once wrote that the appeal of Dean Park was that of 'green foliage against blue skies, of white tenting and bright flags flying, of picnic basket and unfenced boundary'.

On that heady Saturday in 1961 there were nigh on ten thousand spectators rammed into the ground. The travelling Tykes among them were rewarded with a setting that belonged to a different planet from Bramall Lane; not to mention an opening stand of 141 by Bryan Stott and Brian Bolus. Mind you, the newly crowned champions had been somewhat impeded on the first day – by thumping hangovers in some cases. Butch White's obituary in the *Daily Telegraph* mentions in the final paragraph a comment by team-mate Alan Castell on arriving at the ground the morning after the night before: 'The first thing I saw was Butch's car, parked on its own right in the middle of the road. He'd got so pissed someone had to take him home.'

The Duke of Edinburgh's XI at Dean Park in 1949.

White had made a significant contribution to Hampshire's success that season, but his figures in the Derbyshire match had been 0 for 22 in the first innings and 0 for 5 in the second. Well, Butch was a fast bowler and Dean Court was a slow wicket, particularly so when compared to the United Service's Ground in Portsmouth (see page 75). It was the metronomic Derek Shackleton who had skittled out the visitors with 6 for 39 in a second innings that saw Derbyshire all out for 111. This after taking 3 for 70 in the first innings – modest by his standards.

'I remember talking to one of the umpires about that performance,' former Hampshire chairman Brian Ford recalls. 'He pointed out that although Shack only took three wickets in that first innings, he was landing the ball on the same spot every time. And he used that well-worn patch to move the ball off the seam so effectively in the second.

Brian is telling me this in the 'W.G. Grace Room', a much improved space occupying what used to be the home dressing room – gents only at one time. Lord Tennyson, grandson of the poet, who played for Hampshire from 1913 to 1935, would have changed in here, while his valet, Walter Livsey, would have had to sort out his lordship before slipping out to change with the players in what was known as the Cowshed. Livsey doubled as the county's wicketkeeper.

The absurd division between amateur 'gentlemen' and professional 'players' was officially abolished in 1962, but at Hampshire they were all in together well before the MCC's decree. The Old Etonian Ingleby-Mackenzie knew how to build

▶ **Right**: *David Gower on his way out to bat at Dean Park.*

▼ **Below**: *A packed pavilion enclosure at Dean Park.*

team spirit. 'Best social mixer I ever knew,' the old pro Jimmy Gray once told me, fondly recalling times when the skipper would produce crates of Guinness from the boot of his 1930s bull-nosed Morris for the team to celebrate Hampshire victories.

At his home in Southampton, Jimmy still has the match ball with which he took eleven Nottinghamshire wickets at Dean Court. Then he stroked it around for a match-winning 51 in Hampshire's second innings. That was in 1952 when players such as him could be declared man of the match but still be expected to change in the Cowshed.

mature trees. The back gardens of eye-wateringly expensive properties have discreet gates providing access to the ground. 'For many years we issued licences for which the residents paid something like a fiver,' Brian remembers. 'In theory they had to be a member if they wanted to use the back-garden gate. But I don't think the policing was terribly good.'

To one side of the pavilion is a somewhat intrusive block of flats that look to be symptomatic of the late nineties property boom. Very 'nouveau' in this setting. They occupy that part of the boundary where, on county match days, there used to be a

Heaven knows what conditions were like in there because, according to Brian, the quaint Edwardian frontage of this pitch-roofed pavilion harboured changing rooms that left something to be desired by gents, players and even club cricketers such as himself. 'I've changed here and I'm still picking the splinters out of my cricket socks,' he says. 'And as I recall, there was just one shower and one bath.'

Could have been worse; could have been using the away team's dressing room at the back of the building. They were missing any view of the ground. Even on a blustery May day like this one, Dean Park is a treat to look at, encircled as it is by a range of

marquee in which the players could take lunch. As with other cricket festivals, there were many more marquees all around the ground, including a hospitality suite for the lord mayor and the rather more rumbustious beer tent.

Brian had early experience of the latter. Having been brought here first in 1946, aged two weeks, he became a schoolboy member almost as soon as he was old enough to understand the fundamentals of cricket. He would have been in his mid-teens during the first County Championship-winning season and it would have been around that time that he was caught on camera by Southern

Television in his school uniform sampling a lunchtime pint. 'When I got back to school that afternoon,' he recalls, 'I was regarded as a hero.' By his fellow pupils at least. The staff were less impressed, though the head teacher was a cricket man and seems to have looked on the incident with a tolerance that would not have prevailed in many another school in those cane-swishing days.

As for the beer, Ingleby-Mackenzie once said of Dean Park: 'You queued up for a warm pint for ages and queued up just as long to get rid of it.' The second part of that quote is a reference to the cramped and primitive toilets. One end of the ground was officially known as the 'two loos end' because it housed a Ladies that wasn't much better than the Gents, although it was considerably less crowded.

That would have been particularly so on royal wedding day 1981, when Hampshire played Sri Lanka and a huge crowd turned up. All male. By that time Dean Court had developed a lengthy tradition of entertaining international teams from the subcontinent. Younger readers may be surprised to learn that, along with New Zealand, they were referred to as the 'minor countries' back in 1962 when Jimmy Gray's opening partner, Roy Marshall, scored one of his two double centuries here, a blistering 228 against Pakistan.

Little did they know at the time that Pakistan, India and Sri Lanka would become major forces in world cricket – or that within thirty years Dean Court would be hosting minor counties rather than minor countries. Hampshire stopped playing first-class matches here in 1992. By that time Bournemouth had long been a part of Dorset. But that wasn't the reason. As so often, the reason was financial.

'We had the ground on a lease, first from the Cooper-Dean family and then from the Cooper-Dean estate,' Brian explains. 'And we were the only county solely responsible for maintaining more than one ground. All the other outgrounds were owned by a local authority, a club or a school. Hampshire had to maintain this all the year round, providing not only the extra seating required for the four county games we played here every season but also accommodation for the groundsman. We worked out that it was costing us between £35,000 and £45,000 a year.'

Who plays here now? 'Dorset around six times a year and Bournemouth University not much more,' says Ken Maxsted, former assistant head teacher, long-time Hampshire follower and the man who helped to negotiate the transfer of the lease from the county to the university. 'It's a lovely ground but very little happens here,' he adds ruefully after pointing out the Cowshed, now used to house the scorers. Next to it is the spot where Ken used to deliver hospital and independent radio commentaries from an ancient green shed that had once housed the Exchange and Telegraph service. 'I remember the groundsman, Fred Kingston, opening the place up for us for the first time back in the eighties,' he goes on. 'When he levered open the door, the floor was strewn with leaves and tickertape inscribed with pre-war county scores.'

Like Brian, Ken will always have Bournemouth in his memories. It was there that they saw Barry Richards cut loose with a sumptuous 129 in a Gillette Cup match against Lancashire in front of a packed house in 1972. It was here during a John Player game against Yorkshire that the same Richards kept stepping

▲ **Above:** *The Duke of Edinburgh leads out his side in 1949.*

◀ **Left:** *Sunil Gavaskar batting for India at Bournemouth, 1971. Bob Stephenson is keeping wicket.*

outside the leg stump to cut Ray Illingworth's slower than usual off-breaks to the boundary. Illy was not a happy bunny. Nor was Brian Close too tickled when Fred Trueman, playing to the crowd, did his old trick of sneaking away from his fielding position at deep fine leg to try to pinch a swig of a spectator's pint.

It was also here, incidentally, that someone had the bright idea of staging a lottery with a first prize of an over in the nets against Trueman's bowling. Surprise, surprise, there were no takers. Presumably the second prize was two overs facing fiery Fred.

Above all, it was here that they saw Hampshire secure not one but two County Championships. John Arlott was there to witness both occasions. (A Hampshire man born and bred, he more than likely watched cricket in his youth at the evocatively named May's Bounty in his native Basingstoke. The county played a first-class game there as recently as 2010 while the Rose Bowl was hosting a rock concert.)

It was in 1973 that Hampshire landed the title for the second time and,

▼ **Below:** *Outside the Portsmouth pavilion in Hampshire, members might rub shoulders with a rear-admiral or two.*

being the end of the season, the Dean Park festival was in full swing. In those days there was no limit to the number of batting points that a county could accumulate and there came a moment in the match against Gloucestershire that Hampshire had built up so many they simply couldn't be caught. Arlott spotted that earlier than most and proclaimed (away from the microphone): 'Gentlemen, I'm declaring that we've won it and I think we should have a party tonight.' He then reached for his trusty briefcase in which he tended to lug around three bottles of very acceptable claret.

For the second time in twelve years, lemonade was not really an option.

THE UNITED SERVICES GROUND, PORTSMOUTH

It was ten past six and the shadows were lengthening over the United Services Ground, Portsmouth, on a late August day in 1956. Imagine for a moment how it felt to be the young and inexperienced Ray Flood as a wicket fell and he pulled on his gloves. Waiting to greet Hampshire's number six was Frank 'Typhoon' Tyson of Northamptonshire and England, one of the fastest bowlers in the world at the time.

Alan Rayment, who batted number four and was already back in the pavilion, remembers it like this: 'Our captain Neville Rogers put his arm round Ray, who was only five foot six, and said: "Floody,

I want to see you going in to bat again tomorrow morning." Well, Ray took guard and could just about see Tyson at the start of his run-up. He looked behind him and saw that the slips were halfway to the boundary and the wicketkeeper was even further back. The umpire, Harry Baldwin, called out: "How do you feel, Floody?" and back came the answer: "Bloody lonely." But he survived.'

Only to be out for seven the following

morning, alas. Harry Baldwin, incidentally, was the umpire entrusted with a transistor radio by a later Hampshire captain, Colin Ingleby-Mackenzie, to keep him abreast of the racing results. While we can imagine Ingleby-Mackenzie as a graduate of the Mr Toad school of motoring whenever he climbed behind the wheel of his car, the young Rayment was known to his team-mates as Fangio, after the Argentinian racing driver of the 1950s. He hurtled round the Hampshire highways in a 1948 1.5-litre Jaguar, bought from the proceeds of the dancing school that he ran in Southampton, rather than his earnings from cricket, which amounted to £500 a year. Alan liked fast cars and fast wickets and, in that regard, the county's regular visits to Portsmouth suited him fine. 'It wasn't as beautiful as Bournemouth, but it was a lot quicker. I liked the way the way the ball came on to the bat,' he recalls.

Jimmy Gray also liked playing there, despite once taking a nasty blow on the ear from a ball delivered by Surrey's Peter Loader. 'If you got in, there was a good pace,' Jimmy confirms. Well, he certainly 'got in' at Portsmouth in 1962, contributing 213 not out to Hampshire's total of 373 against Derbyshire. His opening partner Roy Marshall evidently took a shine to the United Services pitch as well, totalling 549 over the five county matches played there in 1957.

A fast pitch also suits fast bowlers, as another Marshall showed to devastating effect during Portsmouth's cricket week in 1990. After turning in match figures of 9 for 94 against Nottinghamshire, Malcolm of that ilk put their East Midlands neighbours to the sword with seven wickets in fifty-one balls in Derbyshire's second innings. The local press described it as Marshall's 'finest hour', although, as one or two England batsmen might recall with a wince, he'd had quite a few fine ones for the West Indies.

So what made the United Services Ground such a pacey place to play? For a start, Portsmouth is built on chalk. 'Butch White, who was used to following through on the softer, uncovered wickets that were common in those days, complained that his shins and ankles ached like nobody's business after a week here,' says Hampshire historian Dave Allen. Apart from that, this ground harboured what was surely the heaviest roller in county cricket. Went by the name of Hercules, and it was groundsman Bob Wheldon's pride and joy – particularly useful for flattening that part of the outfield shared with the United Services Rugby Club. But after county cricket ceased here at the dawn of the twenty-first century, the Ministry of Defence trundled Hercules off to Aldershot.

By that time, the opening of the Rose Bowl was only a summer away and the days of the county splitting their matches between Southampton, Portsmouth and Bournemouth was a distant memory. Apart from anything else, there had been something of a deterioration of the flat, true United Services wicket during the nineties. Hercules, unchained rather too often, was thought to be compacting the soil so much that the grass roots didn't reach down far enough, thereby producing a thatching effect.

That's one theory. Certainly the two rollers leaning against a wall near the pavilion are comparative lightweights. The pavilion itself is a venerable building of peeling paintwork with some stone facing here and there. 'I'm sure there used to be red brick under that stone,' ponders Dave, who ought to know. He lives just around the corner and has been coming here, man and boy, since 1959. 'I was ten at the time and I must have been getting under my mother's feet during the long school holidays,' he recalls. '"Why don't you go and watch the cricket?" she suggested.'

Ah, those innocent days when children didn't have to be ferried everywhere by their parents.

'We were playing Surrey at the time,' Dave goes on. 'Lock, Laker, Bedser and Loader: all the stars were out, apart from Peter May who wasn't playing for some reason. The first wicket I saw here was John Edrich lbw to [Derek] Shackleton for a duck.' He also witnessed a comparatively rare phenomenon – a fast hundred from Ken Barrington as Surrey chased 278 to win and fell just short on 266 for 9.

No wonder Dave fell in love with cricket that scorching August. His long association with Hampshire makes him well enough known to get us through the high-security entrance system that has

replaced a much more imposing portal to the ground. The King James's Gate now appears to be purely ornamental. It was transferred here in 1860 from 'Spice Island', a part of town packed with pubs and brothels.

Portsmouth has a long seafaring tradition, of course. Dockyard workers and naval ratings in their white summer hats made up a large part of the crowds that turned out for county games in Dave's youth. 'The dockers became quite voluble as the day went on and the beer went down,' he recalls.

They would sit around the perimeter on wooden benches. Outside the pavilion, meanwhile, Hampshire members might find themselves rubbing shoulders with a rear admiral or two. 'They all sat on what you might call church-hall chairs,' recalls Carol Cooper who is scoring for this afternoon's match between the Royal Navy Under-25s and a team called Havant Wednesdays, founded by shopkeepers on their afternoon off.

Carol, too, has long memories of a ground where she was first brought by her grandfather as a child – 'oh, the smell of steam trains and Brickwood's Brewery.' She would have been there in August 1968, when Barry Richards hit 206 in a day against Notts. And she would have been part of a crowd of around eight thousand that turned up for a John Player Sunday League game against Essex the following year. Hampshire lost heavily but still finished runners-up to Lancashire.

'My dad was a member of the Officers' Club,' she says, pointing to a building with a curved, glazed frontage at the opposite end from the pavilion. 'He'd been a flight lieutenant which meant that he was one of the few RAF members among all those naval chaps. What I remember is being allowed to sit out on the balcony and watch the cricket when I was seventeen.'

The building is now owned by Portsmouth University, like many another in the busy streets around the ground. Students are far more prevalent in the town today than sailors and dockyard workers.

Well, times change and so do cricket pitches. The once highly regarded Portsmouth track had deteriorated to such an extent by 1999 that the county stayed away for the first time since 1895. They returned for one final festival the following year, losing first to New Zealand A, then to Kent and finally to Middlesex in a one-day game.

No less a player than Rahul Dravid scored the final first-class century on the ground. He was playing for Kent at the time while Shane Warne was in the Hampshire side. Warne against 'the Wall': some contest. On this occasion 'the Wall' won. 'Eventually Dravid was dislodged by Giles White, a part-time leg-spinner, who's now our county coach,' says Dave, who, as chairman of the Portsmouth area supporters' club, felt privileged to be watching with Sir Colin Cowdrey a few months before his death. 'It may have been the last game he saw,' he muses. 'Certainly it was sublime cricket,' he adds with the tone of regret that you might expect from a man who knew that he had watched his beloved Hampshire play their final first-class match at his beloved Portsmouth.

Their chances of coming back seem about as remote as Hercules being airlifted into Lord's.

◀ **Left**: *The United Services Ground.*

J. SAMUEL WHITE'S GROUND, COWES, ISLE OF WIGHT

Trevor Bailey travelled considerable distances to represent England in the Test-match arena. Only once, however, did he step off the British mainland while playing for Essex on the county circuit. The year was 1961; the venue was J. Samuel White's Ground, named for and owned by a shipping company in Cowes on the Isle of Wight; the opposition, needless to say, was Hampshire and the match was eventful to put it mildly.

Essex batted for most of the first day and T.E. Bailey enjoyed a lengthy fourth-wicket partnership with the South African Joe Milner. 'This was not to the liking of Gubby Allen, the Chairman of Selectors, who had come down to have a look at Barry Knight,' Bailey recalled in his book *I've Been Everywhere*,

Man. 'Why he should have picked Cowes as a place to judge a quick bowler I never did discover. Worse was to come. Barry, keen to impress Gubby, came charging up to bowl after my declaration, pulled a muscle in his second over and was unable to bowl again in that match.'

Bailey and his team-mate Ken Preston showed shrewder judgement that Saturday evening by choosing Hampshire captain Colin Ingleby-Mackenzie as their guide to the best pubs and clubs on the island. 'Around 11 p.m. we ran into one of his vast collection of acquaintances . . . He suggested that we might like a few drinks on his yacht in the harbour. Having been rowed out to the yacht, Ken and I sipped a beer on deck while our host went back to fetch Colin in the dinghy.'

They watched as he prepared to step aboard the yacht at exactly the same moment as the dinghy

gesturing towards the Downs on our left, 'and seating where those concrete terraces are,' he adds, tilting his cuppa to the right. 'There were nearly seven thousand people here on the first day of a Championship decider against Essex in August 1978,' he goes on. Which suggests that the county must have had to supply temporary seating every time there was a festival.

'They did. And that was part of the problem in the end. It was costing them too much.'

Bear in mind that, at one time, Kent had outgrounds all the way from south-east London to the south-east coast, taking in Maidstone, Gravesend, Dartford and Tonbridge on the way. Not to mention the Nevill Ground at Tunbridge Wells, now hosting the only festival outside Canterbury. Bear in mind also that when they bade farewell to Folkestone, four-day cricket was underway and the number of fixtures was being reduced.

John evidently hasn't entirely given up hope that they'll return one day. Kent chief executive Jamie Clifford has apparently made encouraging noises about the new pavilion and, indeed, the pitch since it was recently relaid. The county second team has already played a couple of Twenty20 games here. But John is also a realist. 'It takes a while for a new wicket to bed in,' he concedes, 'so I'm not expecting the county first team to come back any time soon.'

Meanwhile, Folkestone's older cricket lovers have their memories to live on. Most would have enjoyed watching Gary Sobers score 123 in 1970, even if it did enable Nottinghamshire to declare on 376 for 4. But they probably savoured Brian Luckhurst's 156 not out even more. It led the way to an unlikely three-wicket victory that put them in sight of something very special. In the second festival game at Cheriton Road, they inflicted an innings defeat on Leicestershire. Two games and two wins in quick succession. Kent had been bottom of the table in early July. But after leaving Folkestone at the end of August, they were well on their way to landing the County Championship for the first time since 1913.

◀ **Left:** *The old pavilion at Folkestone.*

The letter is dated 30 June. No year is given, but we can assume that it must have been 2000 because the signatory, one Colin Cowdrey, took over the presidency of Kent CCC at the end of the millennium and came back to Maidstone for at least half of the four-day game against Somerset. 'The Mote was at its old-fashioned best,' he wrote, 'and I enjoyed my two days more than any other of my year as president. True cricket on a perfect Kent ground . . . What a thrill . . . '

The recipient of this heartfelt missive was Bill Deedes, former editor of the *Daily Telegraph*, legendary foreign correspondent and one of those columnists you had to read whether you agreed with his views or not. Bill had briefly played for Hampshire in his youth, but he was a resident of Kent and he duly sent on the letter to Tony Levick, chairman of Maidstone at the time and still a trustee. He, in turn, passed it on to Malcolm Bristow whose days as groundsman at the Mote were coming to an end after 38 years. The letter is still one of his prized possessions, judging by the way he carefully puts it back in its envelope.

On an overcast Sunday morning in 2013 we're standing outside the pavilion, built in 1910, half-timbered, balconied and handsomely tiled, with a huge clock dominating the central gable. Cowdrey came down the steps of that pavilion at the beginning of July 1973, conscious that he had never scored a century here at what he had regularly assured Malcolm was one of his top three grounds in the world ('another was Lord's and the third was somewhere in Australia, I think.') Batting at number six, he hit 123 not out against Somerset. 'That was the 99th of his career,' Malcolm goes on. 'I remember telling him: "You've got another match this week, so you could get your hundredth hundred at the Mote." He said: "Oooh, I'd love that".'

Sometimes you get what you wish for and, in this case, what you deserve. Batting at number seven against Surrey, Cowdrey finished on exactly 100 not out and duly joined the pantheon. Apart from Lord's, one suspects, there's nowhere he would rather have marked that remarkable feat. Sadly, he died towards the end of his presidency, in December 2000, but at least those sublime two days revisiting Mote Park were comparatively fresh in his memory.

Five summers later, and five years after Malcolm's retirement, a low-scoring game against Gloucestershire was over in two days and the 'home' side were deducted eight points as a result. An overwatered 'green' wicket was named as the culprit and, as a result, Mote Park joined the lengthy list of former Kent outgrounds. All this after 140 consecutive visits.

What Sir Colin would have made of it we can only speculate. The Kent ground that he most loved remains largely as it was. For the time being at least. To our right is the so-called Tabernacle, originally the private pavilion of Viscount Bearsted, who had the ground laid out next to his stately pile and country house park in 1908. The Tabernacle is small but beautifully formed with ornate brickwork, all sorts of decorative gables and a veranda with a white-painted balustrade. His lordship apparently used it to entertain his private guests, rather as businesses now use marquees for corporate entertainment.

There was, needless to say, many a marquee around the Mote at festival time. Not quite enough for one Kent official who once asked Malcolm about the chances of 'cutting down that oak tree' to accommodate one more. To his credit, the groundsman refused. Oak trees dominate the far end of the ground, but the one the official had in mind was (and still is) the pick of the bunch – an ancient, spreading oak big enough to have accommodated not only Charles II but probably an entire platoon of fleeing cavaliers had it been in Worcester rather than Maidstone.

The rural, unspoilt nature of the ground is under threat from redevelopment. Plans are afoot to build houses on at least part of the rugby pitch that currently nestles discreetly to the right of the oaks. That would help to finance the demolition of the current pavilion and its replacement by something with twenty-first-century facilities, as happened in nearby Folkestone (see above). But there is obviously some friction over the plans, both within Maidstone CC and between the cricket club and the local rugby club.

While waiting for Malcolm, I just happened to bump into Steve Merwood, a member of the cricket committee who is against the plans, partly because he doesn't want to see a beautiful, historic cricket ground losing some of its appeal. 'There will also be new roadways around the ground and at least two of the oaks will go,' he told me. 'Those who are in favour think the new pavilion will encourage Kent to come back. But the likelihood of that is remote given that they've just spent six million down at Canterbury.'

▼ **Below:** *Maidstone in the early days.*

Did the Kent players object to the facilities in the current pavilion?

'They were prepared to put up with the changing rooms and, over the years, they've had some excellent games of cricket here.'

Only ten years before the county bade farewell to Maidstone, Aravinda de Silva and another Cowdrey, Colin's grandson Graham, overtook Kent's highest partnership for any wicket in first-class cricket. They put on 368 against Derbyshire. And in the same year, Mark Ealham scored the fastest century in the history of the forty-over game. He reached his hundred in 44 balls with nine sixes and nine fours.

Perhaps the most memorable one-day match at the Mote, however, was in 1976. On the final Sunday of the John Player League, any one of five counties was in with a chance of winning it. 'The BBC had a helicopter travelling around between the grounds with the trophy on board, and it was still quite a way away when Kent finally won it,' Malcolm recalls. 'I'd been asked to mark out a pad for them to land on the bottom rugby pitch. But Peter Walker, who was commentating, said: "We'll be going off air soon; they'll just have to land on the square."'

And so they did.

I can think of a few groundsmen who would have had an attack of the vapours in such a situation, but Malcolm took it in his stride. 'It didn't do much damage,' he shrugs. 'But I did have to go down the police station to explain why we'd allowed a helicopter to land. The local police chief had been watching on telly and he was concerned about the size of the crowd on the pitch at the time it descended. Anyway, I gave a statement and heard nothing more about it. They weren't so obsessed with health and safety in those days.'

In those days, after all, cigarette companies were allowed to sponsor major cricket tournaments.

▶ **Right:** *Mote Park drew big crowds to watch Kent.*

THE RECTORY FIELD, BLACKHEATH

The Rectory Field seems a long way from Folkestone and Maidstone. Or Canterbury for that matter. It's also some distance from the middle of Blackheath. After a lengthy hike from Westcombe Park station, I finally track it down on the borders of Charlton. We are also somewhere near what was once the boundary between Kent and Surrey.

Local derbies between those two great cricketing rivals began in 1889 and became an annual fixture in 1906. Other counties had a look-in every now and then, but Kent v. Surrey was the major draw year after year. It was here that Hobbs and Hayward's opening partnership for Surrey amounted to 234 in August 1914, shortly before the outbreak of the First World War. Twenty years later, Fagg and Woolley put on 219 for Kent. By that time, Woolley would have been 47 years old. He scored 2,049 runs at Blackheath in 31 matches.

Eight bombs fell on the Rectory Field during the Second World War – mainly on the nearby tennis courts, although one came close to destroying the half-timbered pavilion. Luckily, it and the ground survived to stage some memorable matches in the post-war years. Tony Lock took 16 Kent wickets for 83 in 1956 and, three years later, Colin Cowdrey stroked his way to 250 when Essex made a rare visit.

'Big crowds used to turn up in the fifties and sixties,' says Chris Swadkin, chairman of Blackheath CC's junior section, who still turns out for the Kent over-60s side. 'There was a long stand running all the

In my admittedly limited experience of Blackpool itself, real ale has been something of a rarity. The nearest thing I found to draught on most visits was the 'draught champagne' at the late lamented Yates's Wine Lodge. Yet the pavilion here has been voted Lancashire and North-West Camra Club of the Year. Time, perhaps, to break the habit of a recent lifetime and savour a pint on a Monday lunchtime.

Looks good, tastes good and, by golly, it slips down a treat while I take in the comfortable, spacious and well-polished surroundings. Among the photographs on walls and pillars is one of a crowd of anything between 10,000 and 13,000 that gathered here in August 1950 to see Lancashire defeat Glamorgan by an innings and 70 runs with Malcolm Hilton taking 6 for 52 in the visitors' second innings. Many spectators are standing and one or two appear to be peering over the sightscreen while clinging on like grim death. There would, of course, be many a holidaymaker in that crowd yet knotted handkerchiefs are difficult to spot, in the foreground at least.

Nearby is a photo of Hanif Mohammad, the 'Little Master' long before Sachin Tendulkar, and one of many distinguished professionals to grace the Blackpool club side. The most legendary of all is honoured by a blue plaque on the pavilion's exterior, next to one of several doors made weatherproof by uPVC. Harold Larwood kept a sweet shop in the town and was the pro here in 1939 until Adolf Hitler called close of play for a while. During his short stay, Larwood took 68 wickets, most of them clean bowled, at an average of 10.57.

Other Blackpool pro's included the rumbustious Bill Alley and hooker extraordinaire Rohan Kanhai. Collis King and Richie Richardson came later. But perhaps the most influential, when it came to links with Old Trafford, was Jack Simmons.

His nickname, 'Flat Jack', had more to do with his bowling action than his physique, nourished as it was by a prodigious consumption of pie and chips. Nonetheless, he played on until his late forties before going into administration and becoming chairman of Lancashire.

Green trees and a two-tiered pavilion set the perfect county cricket scene.

It was obviously a coincidence that his departure to the England and Wales Cricket Board in 2008 coincided with four days' rain at Stanley Park, which washed out the match against Surrey, leading as it did to a flood of almost biblical proportions. Blackpool chairman Dave Cresswell evidently believes that Flat Jack always had a soft spot for Blackpool and had some influence over the county's continued visits for so many years. So was it just a coincidence that the ground has been granted no more than one match since he left for the ECB – and that in 2011 when Old Trafford was undergoing major redevelopment? The county hasn't been back since.

'That washout in 2008 cost us about fifteen grand,' Dave recalls, almost with a shudder. 'We'd had some issues with the drainage of the outfield. The drains ran out into the putting green in the park on the other side of the wall, but the ground is lower than the green and water finds its level. It started flowing back. The fire brigade were here at one point, pumping it out.'

It probably didn't help Blackpool's cause that, two years earlier, some kids had fired a water bomb from the adjoining park. With uncanny accuracy, it landed smack on the wicket and disrupted the game against Warwickshire for a while.

Anyway, Dave points out that the club has invested in a better drainage system since 2008. They also have a new groundsman who has prepared a first-class wicket. All that they've been lacking for the past year or two is first-class cricket. 'Matt Merchant [groundsman at Old Trafford] hasn't been out here at the end of the season for the past couple of years and that tells me something,' says the Blackpool chairman, ruefully.

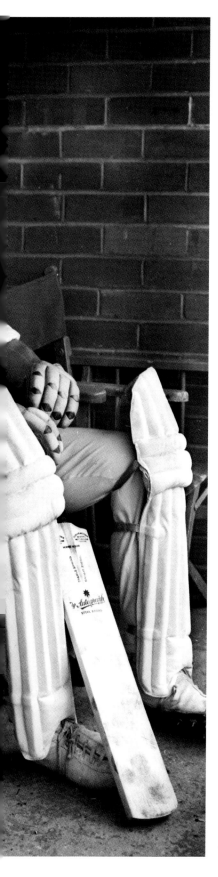

▲ **Previous pages**: *Lancashire v Glamorgan at Stanley Park 1949. Even more turned up the following year.*

▶ **Right**: *Cyril Washbrook and Jack Ikin walk out at Stanley Park in 1953.*

◀ **Left**: *Frank Hayes waiting for a wicket to fall in 1970.*

◀ **Far left**: *The Lancashire team at Blackpool 1932.*

At this point we're joined by Gerry Wolstenholme, sporting green corduroy trousers and a baseball cap bearing the message: 'I love cup cakes'. It's not the sort of gear that he would have worn back in the 1960s when he was a civil servant at the Treasury. Having lived in London for twelve years, he returned to his home town and remains a champion of Blackpool in general and Stanley Park in particular. Indeed, he's the club historian.

'Our attendances here were always the best in the County Championship for Lancashire,' he insists. 'The only one that rivalled us was the Roses match at Old Trafford. Yet the county won't come back.'

But they have spent a lot of money on Old Trafford, I point out.

'Still they went back to [Trafalgar Road] Southport where I once saw a bloke calling for a scorecard from a deckchair in his back garden.' And Aigburth, Liverpool? 'They've always gone there, even though they don't get as good crowds as they did here.'

Dave interjects: 'From the players' point of view, though, they have almost exclusive use of the pavilion there. They like to keep themselves to themselves. Also they've relaid the wicket at Aigburth and it's a nice one to play on.'

Gerry nods as though conceding that he might have a point. But don't get him started on the decision to play at Church Road, Lytham St Annes, from 1985 to 1998. Of course, Lancashire's decision may well have had something to do with Blackpool staging a joint benefit match for Ian Botham and Geoffrey Boycott in 1984 (long before Dave's chairmanship) without consulting county headquarters. Stanley Park was cut out of the first-class fixture list for the next six years.

Lytham is seven miles up the coast from Blackpool and – how can we put this? – somewhat more refined. Though born in Preston, a promising youngster called Andrew Flintoff emerged from this unlikely setting. But he played for the town's other club, St Annes. 'I got him out once,' Dave recollects. 'He was twelve at the time.'

That would have been around 1989. Gerry, meanwhile, is taking us back to his own childhood in the 1950s when he would set off to watch county matches at Stanley Park with his sandwiches, his bottle of pop and sometimes his father in tow. 'The first game I went to with Dad would have been around 1955. I remember walking past the scoreboard and next minute the ball thumped into it.

"Crapp," said Dad.

"It looked pretty good to me."

"No, Jack Crapp of Gloucestershire. He's the one who hit it."'

Smiting sixes on an outfield this size was nowhere near as easy as on some outgrounds I can think of. Gerry remembers one of my boyhood heroes, Jim Stewart of Warwickshire, setting about the Lancashire bowling with some relish in 1959. In two innings he cleared the boundary rope sixteen times. 'At least one of them finished up in the street,' Gerry remembers. 'Jack Dyson went for about 45 in three overs and Malcolm Hilton didn't do much better.' At least Hilton finally caught Stewart off Ken Higgs, but by that time he's made 155. In the second innings, he scored 125 to no avail. The match was drawn.

Brian Statham was a notable absentee from the Lancashire side that day. Maybe he was on Test match duty. 'I lost count of the times he took five wickets or more on this ground,' Gerry confides. 'But he was also brilliant in the field. He used to stand not far from us on that boundary and his throw was tremendous at a time when fielding wasn't anywhere near as good as it is today.'

Alas, young Wolstenholme was a little too young in 1953 to see Bob Berry take all ten wickets in Worcestershire's second innings as Lancashire won by 18 runs. Still, he had many a treat in store as those long-ago summers unfolded – not least an invitation to the Ladies' Pavilion, if you please. 'You had to be invited in by a lady in those days, and one of the older ones said to me: "Do you want to come in for your tea?" Well, it was fantastic. There were table cloths and pastry forks.' Whatever was served at afternoon tea dances at the Tower Ballroom, it seems, had nothing on those spreads.

▲ **Above:** *Clive Lloyd in 1970: He never scored a century at Blackpool.*

◀ **Left:** *A big holiday crowd with not a knotted handkerchief in sight.*

The building is still there, looking very 1930s. It's not as attractive as the Ladies' Pavilion at Worcester and, unlike Worcester's, it's no longer a purveyor of tea and home-made cakes. These days it hosts a kindergarten but, until fairly recently, it had another function on the days when Lancashire came a-calling. 'It became the home team's changing room,' Dave assures me. 'We had to re-tile the floor to accommodate them. The changing rooms here are big by club standards but not spacious enough for players used to Old Trafford. They like to be separated from the other team and they don't really like mingling with the spectators.'

That would have been the case when Mike Atherton scored 268 not out here in 1999 and, more surprisingly, in the seventies and early eighties when his commentary box buddy David Lloyd scored three centuries here, one fewer than Alan Wharton did in 1949 and the 1950s. Surprisingly, Bumble's namesake Clive Lloyd never quite made a hundred here.

'Even in Clive's day,' says Dave, 'the players tended to get in their cars at the end of a day's play and head back to the Imperial Hotel rather than stay here for a drink.'

Well, I hope the beer was as good as it is in the Stanley Park pavilion bar today. Though somehow I doubt it.

LEICESTERSHIRE

OAKHAM SCHOOL

Not many professional cricketers get the chance to play their first County Championship match on the playing fields of the school they left the previous year. But that's what happened to Stuart Broad when he turned out for Leicestershire against Somerset at Oakham on the not-so-glorious first of June 2005. Day one was lost to rain. There to watch him on days two, three and four were at least three former England Test players – his father, Chris, as well as Frank Hayes, then master in charge of cricket at Broad's alma mater, and David Steele, who also coached there. Phil de Freitas may well have been looking on as well. Certainly he'd had a hand in the lanky lad's development.

No pressure then, Stuart?

Silly question. If you can't cope with pressure, you don't become a regular Test player yourself. Broad may not have lived up to his promise as a great all-rounder but, on his day, he's a very fine bowler, as those of us witnessed his series-changing hat-trick against India at Trent Bridge in 2011 will testify.

So how did he do in that first county match in surroundings that must have seemed very familiar? Better than his figures (2 for 21 and 1 for 40) suggest, perhaps. Over to you, Mr Hayes: 'He bowled extremely well, particularly before lunch. And against Northants the following year he was coming in at around 85 mph and making it swing away.

He's telling me this as we look out from the pavilion on a chilly Monday morning while the wind whips across acres of wide-open playing fields and rattles the wire wrapped around the flagless flagpole pole outside. Not that it's cold in here.

Oakham has sporting facilities
that few schools can match.

With a few beer pumps and a log fire, Ye (not so) Olde Pavilion could be a rather pleasant pub. There are solid wooden tables and some handsome high-backed settles overlooking the field of play. Once inside it's difficult to believe that this used to be the school gymnasium. The building was converted to its current use as recently as 1983. It feels much older. There are weathered, signed cricket bats around the walls and large wooden plaques commemorating the school's lengthy association with first-class cricket. There was another, thatched pavilion that burnt down in 1972, and it would have been under that thatch that players from Warwickshire, Derbyshire and Kent (twice) found themselves changing back in the 1930s.

Oakham itself is just down the road. It's a pleasant, rather quaint town in the smallest county in England. Relations between Rutland and big brother Leicestershire have not always been convivial, particularly in 1974 when local government changes lumped one in with the other. Since then Rutland has declared itself independent again, but there remains a Leicestershire and Rutland Cricket Board and Rutland has a unique place in the game's history. Some two miles from Oakham is Burley-on-the-Hill, home to a family of Finches. George Finch, the ninth Earl of Winchilsea, is regarded as the chief founder of the MCC in 1787. In the 1790s he arranged matches in Burley Park involving, among others, the cricket creators of Hambledon. An All-England side visited nearby Uppingham in 1854 and there were ten fixtures between Rutland and the MCC, beginning in 1881. Leicestershire seconds have played there much more recently.

Only Oakham School, though, has hosted first-class cricket in Rutland.

Surprisingly, perhaps, it didn't feature on a lengthy list of outgrounds that Leicestershire used in the 1940s and 1950s before Grace Road became the county's permanent headquarters. They visited Hinckley, Coalville, Barwell, Loughborough, Melton Mowbray and Ashby de la Zouch (see page 106). But not until the dawning of the new century did they venture back to Oakham.

As so often, it was somebody with connections who made the . . . er, connection. In this case it was Brian 'Milky' Smith, president of the club, head of a Leicester dairy company and an Old Oakhamian – one-time captain of cricket and rugby, no less. He would have known the pitch and no doubt have been aware that his old school had a very fine groundsman in Keith Exton.

Frank Hayes rates him highly as well. 'I always made a point of having a beer with Bert Flack at Old Trafford and Harry Brind at the Oval,' he confides, 'and I'd put Keith up there with them.' Praise indeed. 'I once saw him on all fours, using a blowlamp to get rid of some perennial weeds. All top groundsmen have the same work ethic.'

Exton has since been lured away by Glamorgan, the SWALEC Stadium in Cardiff having established itself as a Test match arena. No doubt the word had got around on the circuit that Oakham, unlike some outgrounds the players could mention, had a wicket well worthy of first- class cricket. Certainly Alistair Brown took a liking to it, contributing 295 to Surrey's first innings total of 505 as the away side went on to inflict an innings defeat on their hosts in that first game in 2000.

That might have put Leicestershire off crossing the Rutland border again. But no. 'They liked the pavilion and they liked the festival setting, different as it was from Grace Road,' Frank insists. 'And they liked the wicket.' Particularly Brad Hodge, it would seem, who hit 221 for the home side as they romped to a six-wicket victory over Derbyshire in 2004. Not to mention Virender Sehwag and Tony Ward who had set about the Worcestershire attack with some venom in a one-day game the previous year. Sehwag hit 76 in 59 balls and Ward 68 in 44 to set up a Leicestershire victory by 76 runs.

The county's 'honorary' archivist Richard Holdridge was there for most if not all 'home' games at Oakham, and he's with Frank Hayes and me this morning. 'We had a few gorgeous days here,' he recalls. 'There were lots of tents encircling the pitch and it was easy to slip into town for a bite to eat at lunchtime. My wife also remembers some clay pigeon shooting going on at the far end of the field, well away from the cricket, of course.'

Stepping outside the pavilion this morning, the wind has dropped for a while and it's not difficult to imagine the festival atmosphere here on a fine summer's day. There are mature trees along one side of the ground and a white picket fence fronting a narrow stretch of waterway on the other. Church spires are dotted around hither and yon, one of them seeming to peep over the fives courts next to the sports hall.

Oakham has sporting facilities that few schools can match and those in the state sector could only dream of. But then fees for boarders in the upper and middle school amount to £29,355 a year. Having former Test cricketers on hand appears to be part of the package. (John Crawley has recently taken over cricket coaching from Frank, who now confines himself to teaching physics.) No wonder that, apart from Broad, the school has supplied a steady stream of first-class players to Leicestershire in recent times, including Matt Boyce, Josh Cobb and Alex Wyatt. All the more surprising, then, that the county's trips across the Rutland border should come to an end some eight years after they had resumed.

To find out why perhaps we should consult Frank's former colleague Neil Mullinger, former director of sport at Oakham School and the man who did more than most to organise the annual cricket festival. 'It was a real sadness to me that the chairman of the trustees and the new bursar felt that they could no longer justify the expense,' he reflects. 'My argument was that you couldn't measure the PR value. To put on a four-day game cost us around fifteen grand, less than the

▲ **Above:** *A visiting Kent side in front of the old thatched pavilion in the 1930s.*

annual fee for a non-boarder (£17,625). I know of one cricket lover who was travelling down the A1 listening to the lunchtime scores on his radio. On hearing that there was a first-class match being played here, he made a diversion to watch the afternoon's play and finished up sending his daughter to Oakham.'

Now teaching maths part-time at a local academy, Neil looks back fondly on the days when he felt that the hard work of planning for Leicestershire's visits seemed well worth it. 'It was like having first-class cricket in your front garden, as my office was right up against the boundary.'

Luckily the windows survived the day Sehwag and Ward were in full flow; the ball was flying to all parts of Rutland and even distant pigeons felt glad to be clay.

THE BATH GROUNDS, ASHBY DE LA ZOUCH

Although Jack Firth of Leicestershire was never up there in the top rank of wicketkeeper batsmen, he could always claim to have hit a ball that travelled just short of eighteen miles. It started on the Bath Grounds at Ashby de la Zouch and finished up in Leicester. Admittedly it was conveyed by a goods train that chugged past shortly after Jack had clouted a six back over the bowler's head and cleared the old ramshackled pavilion that used to stand at the railway end of the ground. The boundary was comparatively short by first-class standards and putting one on the line was a fairly regular occurrence, particularly when the counties came out to play.

Leicestershire visited twice a year from 1912 to 1964. They always played near-neighbours Derbyshire (the boundary was a mile and a half up the road) and A.N. Other-shire as part of a week-long festival. Firth's flyer would have embarked on its lengthy journey in the 1950s, a few years before Dr Beeching set about his axe-work. 'Trains stopped play' was not unheard of at Ashby, particularly if the driver of those old steam engines chose to stop and watch for a while, emitting clouds of smoke in the process.

There are no trains now and the former station building is occupied by an insurance broker. But the imposing entrance to Ashby Hastings Cricket Club is still sharp right under the railway bridge if approaching from the south. At the end of the tree-lined track you come to the wide open spaces of the Bath Grounds, cricket pitch in the foreground, sightscreens in place, dog-walkers prowling the boundary, crows pecking over a freshly mown wicket. It's a fine last day of April and the promise of a long season to come hangs in the late spring air.

Old-timers with long memories will tell you that the 'grounds', rather like the nearby Royal Hotel, have seen better days. The classical colonnade of the old bath buildings that gave Ashby the status of spa town is no longer visible. They've been demolished. Gone, too, is the view of the castle – not because it has been demolished as well but because the trees over the bowls club are now tall enough to obscure it from view.

▼ **Below:** *The Bath Grounds drew big crowds from the surrounding collieries.*

▶ **Opposite top:** *The railway line where trains sometimes stopped play.*

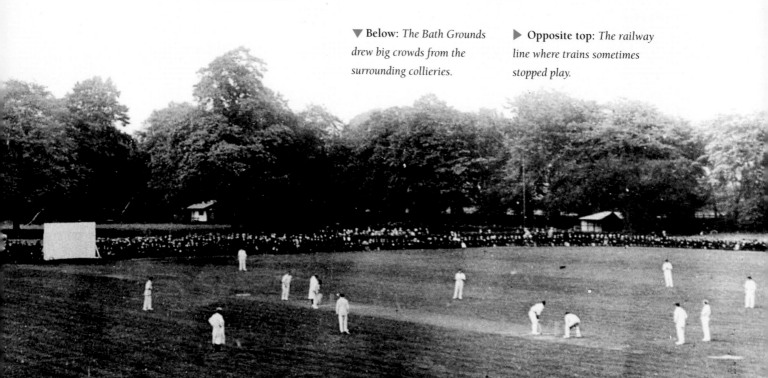

Ashby Castle is the seat of the Hastings family which gave its name to the club. The fourth Marquis of Hastings (1841–67) was not only president but also a batsman who could apparently hit the ball with considerable force. However, he disdainfully refused to run on those occasions when his shots fell short of the boundary. Having lost the match for his side, he would make up for it by treating his team-mates to large quantities of liquid refreshment.

That hospitable tradition continued into the twentieth century, by which time the owner of the Royal Hotel was the one with the deep pockets. Chap by the name of Richard Derrington-Fenning in the 1950s. Wore pinstripes and drove a yellow Rolls-Royce by all accounts. Mike Turner remembers his dealings with him with great pleasure, first as a Leicestershire player and then as the youngest secretary in the County Championship. 'He always recommended the monkey-gland steak,' Mike recalls. 'Heaven knows what it was, but it was delicious.'

And that was just the main course – one of four, including a cheese board, when the Royal put on lunch for the players during festival week. 'Bottles of beer were laid on as well as soft drinks,' he goes on. Any wine? 'Only for the top table where the managers and captains sat.' If it had been down to Derrington-Fenning, they might well have been passing the port by mid-afternoon. But this was the lunch break during a first-class match, remember. Mike beams at the memory. 'We had to extend the break from forty

minutes to an hour.' Then the players would trudge back through the hotel's Japanese gardens, through a little gate and onto the ground where a sizeable crowd would be waiting expectantly.

No wonder the estimable Mr Turner looks back on Ashby as his favourite of Leicestershire's many outgrounds – eleven of them in the period from the end of the Second World War until the early 1960s when he finally secured Grace Road, Leicester, as the county's permanent home. It wasn't just the hospitality that made the Bath Grounds so appealing. 'I always looked forward to Ashby cricket week,' he says. 'It was the kind of place where you could imagine the vicar propping his bike against one of the many trees.'

Very different from visiting Snibston Colliery in the aptly named Coalville, as you might expect. If the batsman started patting down the pitch there, he and short leg would be covered in coal dust. 'There was a slag heap running down one side of the ground,' Mike remembers. 'When the wind was in a certain direction and you were fielding in the covers, it was like breathing in sulphur. Good wicket, mind you. I remember Willie Watson getting a hundred there despite playing with a broken finger.'

Watson was a gritty character, as he proved in 1953 when he and Trevor Bailey saved the Lord's Test for England against Australia and against all the odds. Six years later, Watson hit 109 in the first innings at Ashby and 74 not out in the second as

Leicestershire romped home by eight wickets against Middlesex. His England partner in defiance was part of the Essex team that played here in 1954 when a youthful M.J.K. Smith shared a stand of 159 for Leicestershire with Maurice Tompkin.

'I played against Maurice once in the days when the pros would sometimes come here to play on a Sunday,' Ashby Hastings veteran Phil Aston recalls. '"I'm going to do a Bradman on you," he said, and duly hit my first five balls for six. But I bowled him on the last ball.'

Phil is a lively eighty-nine-year-old who was once on the books at Wolverhampton Wanderers and Birmingham City. During the war, he flew Lancaster bombers from a base near where a buccaneering Australian pilot called Keith Miller was stationed. 'He was a good 'un. A good bloke, I mean, as well as a good cricketer. Keith stayed at the Royal with the Australian team in 1953 while they were warming up here for the Trent Bridge Test. They enjoyed themselves, but then the local ladies were very

obliging.' Phil guffaws before seeing off his second Scotch of the lunchtime while standing at the bar of the 'new' pavilion. It was built as recently as 1970, square-on to the wicket. The rather uninspiring exterior is covered in advertisements. One of them, I can't help noticing, is for Specsavers, 'official opticians to Ashby Hastings CC'. For the umpires, perhaps? Hopefully not required by top-order batsmen . . .

'I also played against Les Jackson [Derbyshire and England],' Phil is saying. 'Nearly took my head off, he did.' Along with Cliff Gladwin, his partner in devastation on uncovered wickets, Jackson was one of quite a few Test players who graced the ground at festival time. 'Nearly all the villages round here were pit villages in the years after the war, whether they were in Leicestershire or Derbyshire' Phil reminds me. 'The miners on early shift could do their seven and a quarter hours then come down to the Bath Grounds, get a drink and watch men who'd played for their country.'

The Derbyshire contingent would have enjoyed Donald Carr's 162 not out in 1960. Ted Dexter brought his Sussex team to town the following year. By his imperious standards, he didn't do much with the bat, getting out for one in the first innings and 46 in the second; but he did bring a grim grin to the faces of Ashby members during a teatime interview with Brian Johnston. 'What a lovely setting,' Lord Ted proclaimed. Then, on being asked what he thought of the pavilion, he moved his tongue firmly into his cheek before replying: 'It reminds me of the Long Room at Lord's.'

Yeah, right, as Jonners would never have said. What Maurice Hallam said about it was this: 'The changing room was so small that it was like climbing over an obstacle course. Vic Munden was allocated the task of bringing some six-inch nails to make sure we'd got enough pegs.'*

'It wasn't like the Long Room in my memory,' smiles club president Martin Bowron, one of several old-stagers standing at the bar this lunchtime. 'That's why we had to build this one.' And even 'this one' might be demolished soon under plans to redevelop the Bath Grounds. 'They're going to build five luxury homes beyond that far boundary,' Martin goes on, gesturing to a point in the middle distance which he assures me will be well out of six-hitting range. And is the club in favour of that?

'We are because it means that ownership of the ground passes from the Royal to the council, and they've agreed a much longer lease that will give us the security of tenure we need to rebuild the pavilion.'

None of which will bother the county because Leicestershire staged their last game here fifty years ago. Unfortunately, the Ashby festival of 1964 was an almost total washout. The first game, against Surrey, was abandoned without a ball being bowled. And there was no play at all on the first two days against Derbyshire. On the third day the gate receipts amounted to £7 10s. 9d. (just over £7.50). Not surprisingly, perhaps, only forty-nine people had turned up. This on a ground that had hosted 4,166 on a Saturday in 1949.

From now on a county that had once had eleven outgrounds would play most of its cricket at home in Leicester which, as we know, is just short of eighteen miles from Ashby as the cricket ball flies.

▲ **Above:** *The Bath grounds long before Leicestershire pulled out.*

◀ **Left:** *Les Jackson and Cliff Gladwin could wreak havoc on an uncovered wicket.*

*As told to Stephen Chalke in The Way It Was: Glimpses of English Cricket's Past.

MIDDLESEX

JOHN WALKER'S GROUND, SOUTHGATE

To pop-music lovers of a certain age the Walker Brothers will always be remembered as an American trio who warbled their way through a succession of hit singles in the sixties. Perhaps the best known was 'The Sun Ain't Gonna Shine Any More', which could well have been adopted by long-suffering Lancashire cricket supporters as they gazed forlornly towards the Pennines from the upper reaches of Old Trafford. For supporters of Middlesex there was another set of Walker brothers of more venerable vintage. There were seven of them, united by birth and a family fortune built through the Taylor Walker brewery, and their heyday was the eighteen sixties.

It was in 1864 that they founded the official Middlesex CCC, having already hosted a match between a Middlesex team and Kent at what then went under the somewhat bucolic sounding name of Chapel Fields in Waterfall Road, Southgate. A crowd touching ten thousand at times turned up to see Kent defeated by 78 runs. The Middlesex side included a V.E. Walker, an A.H. Walker, an F. Walker, an A. Walker and a J. Walker. The latter would almost certainly have been John whose name was later immortalised by the Southgate club. After all, he had paid to have the bumpy Chapel Fields surface returfed in the early 1850s.

There would be subsequent visits from a United All-England team and the MCC to play Southgate. But Middlesex would take rather a long time to return for a first-class match, preferring the Cattle Market Ground, Islington, and Prince's Ground, Chelsea, it would seem, before Thomas Lord opened his third and consummate ground in St John's Wood in 1877. In fact, the following century was drawing to a close when the county came back to Southgate, first for a one-day game (Kent again) in 1991 and then for a four-day match against Essex in 1998.

Groundsman Steve Martin could be forgiven for feeling a little apprehensive before that one. Is it possible for him to relax and enjoy it when the county calls in? 'Only after the end of the first morning, so long as one team's not twenty-five for five.' On this occasion Middlesex fared considerably better than that. By the end of the first day they were 170 for no wicket and by the end of the second they were 373 for one, Justin Langer having finally been caught Rollins bowled Irani for 166. Mike Gatting remained undefeated on 180. He was finally out for 241 and the home side were able to declare on 488 for 2. What appears to have been an extraordinary match finished in a draw, Essex themselves having declared at 151 for 3 at the end of the third day, followed on and then followed up with 315 for 9.

A photograph of Gatting and Langer celebrating that opening stand beams down on us from above the bar in the 1960s pavilion that replaced the rather more architecturally pleasing building bequeathed by the Walker brothers. The big windows are wide open in the summer, providing access for fresh air and, on one improbable occasion, a flying cricket ball. It had been belted by Virender Sehwag on his way to making 130 for Leicestershire in a vain attempt to overhaul Middlesex's first-innings total of 620 in 2003. 'The ball bounced on the patio, came straight through the open window and landed in a Middlesex member's lunch,' Steve recalls. 'There used to be stains down there but we've had a new carpet since.'

Gravy stains?

'No, blood. It hit his nose first.'

The poor man must have wished he'd never left Lord's. 'It was nasty,' Steve concedes. 'But he was all right in the end and I think there was some financial compensation.'

The windows are closed today, thank goodness. It's a bleak and blustery Friday lunchtime in early April and no cricket ground looks at its best in such conditions. The covered square is surrounded by football pitches. 'We have to pay the bills,' Steve shrugs. 'To be honest, football does less damage to the outfield than the hockey that we used to stage here. There are fewer divots and we're quite strict when it comes to calling off games if there's heavy rain.'

In a week or two the goalposts will be gone and, hopefully, the skeletal trees that encircle the cricket pitches will be budding with the promise of spring. Come summer it will be difficult to believe that this part of Southgate is within walking distance of a London Underground station. On the Waterfall Road side at least, there's still a decidedly villagey look to the ground with the spire of Christ Church peering over trees in full foliage.

Not that relations between church and club

◀ **Left:** *One of the Walker brothers who gave their name to the ground.*

have always been harmonious. The Lord's Day Observance Society warned that Denis Compton's benefit match in 1949, between Southgate and Middlesex, would be viewed with 'considerable concern and grief'. It went ahead anyway and a bumper Sunday crowd paid a shilling each to get in. But former Southgate member and future QC Sam Silkin warned that in subsequent years it would be advisable not to charge an entrance fee on the Sabbath. And it wasn't until the late seventies that all-day games at the Walker Ground were allowed to start before noon on a Sunday. More recently, reacting to a complaint about the bells chiming during a Sunday League match, the vicar retorted that the beer tent was always sited on the church side of the ground, thereby ensuring that in any photographs the spire would be fronted by an advertisement for Foster's.

At least the promotion of an Australian lager might have made the players from Down Under feel at home. Justin Langer will have enjoyed that first game here and he chipped in with a useful but ultimately futile second innings 61 for Middlesex two years later. On that occasion Middlesex lost by two wickets to Glamorgan in a game where the square behaved very differently from 1998 – on the first day at least. So many wickets went down that Glamorgan captain Steve James complained about it and Middlesex were promptly deducted eight points, much to Langer's voluble grumbles.

Steve Martin shudders at the memory. 'For a groundsman it was your worst nightmare. We had back-to-back four-day games and the first one was completely washed out by rain. We couldn't get on to prepare for the second one. But the pitch had dried out by the second day and it turned out to be a good game of cricket that went right through almost to the end of day four.' Steve James's opening partner Matthew Elliott, another Aussie, hit a second-innings century and Middlesex's eight points were duly reinstated.

There must have been times, however, when the Southgate groundsman felt that he just couldn't win. Hampshire turned up in 2005, Shane Warne among them at a time when his marriage was breaking up. Conscious perhaps of the tabloid reporters prowling the boundary, he managed to stay out in the middle for as long as possible. By the end of the first day he had top-scored for Hants with 93 not out. Warne duly reached his century the following morning – but only just. He had added eight runs before he was caught Shah bowled Betts for 101.

Still, you might have thought that a number nine would be pleased with what turned out to have been only his second first-class century. If so, he had a funny way of showing it, as Steve recalls. 'At lunch he came over, pointed his finger at me and said: "You must be the only groundsman in the world who doesn't ask me if I want a roller." I had to remind him that it had been threatening rain all morning and we'd had to leave the covers on. Suddenly, at eleven o'clock prompt, the umpires decided to start. There'd been no time to roll the pitch. After a bit more finger-jabbing from him, I told him to eff off back to Australia.'

And what happened next?

'He stormed off. The following day I apologised to him and him to me. "You can understand the pressure I'm under," he said.'

Warne had a better game with the bat than the ball, finishing with figures

of 2 for 57 in the first innings and 2 for 108 in the second as Middlesex went on to win by two wickets. 'It never used to be a spinner's wicket,' Steve goes on. 'It might turn a bit early on but never got any worse.' Judging by his figures, even Southgate's own Phil Tufnell didn't exactly set the Walker Ground on fire when he returned to his first club with Middlesex. But he did live up to his reputation in another respect by inadvertently providing a fine photo opportunity. 'The Cat', as he was known in his home dressing room, duly fell fast asleep in one of the armchairs set out in the corner of the ground, outside Steve's handsome grace-and-favour house. The pictorial evidence is not only published here but has also appeared in *The Cricketer Magazine* as well as a handsomely produced brochure that marked Southgate's 150th birthday in 2005.

It would have been in the previous year that a fifteen-year-old Steven Finn was in Southgate to study his bowling hero and inspiration. Glenn McGrath, Warne's partner in mesmerising England sides for more than a decade, was making a rare appearance for Middlesex in a one-day game against Yorkshire. 'From side-on I could see the incredible carry that he was getting, sending the ball firing through to the wicketkeeper,' Finn eulogised in an article for *All Our Cricket* magazine. 'From behind his arm I could see the "shape" he was getting on the ball, taking it consistently away from the right-hander.'

There was also a four-day match at Southgate that summer. Against Kent, as it happens. McGrath finished with figures of 4 for 59 in the first innings and 1 for 71 in the second. While fielding in the deep, he had what the following day's *Independent* described as 'a snatched conversation' with a 'fan' during which one of the greatest pace bowlers of them all remarked: 'This is the flattest track in the world.' Asked if he was going to take a second-innings wicket, he replied: 'No, I'm saving them all up for England.' The wicket that he *did* take was

◀ **Top:** *Chad Keegan fielding at the Walker Ground: Middlesex v Derbyshire in 2007.*

◀ **Bottom:** *Phil 'the Cat' Tufnell lives up to his name at Southgate.*

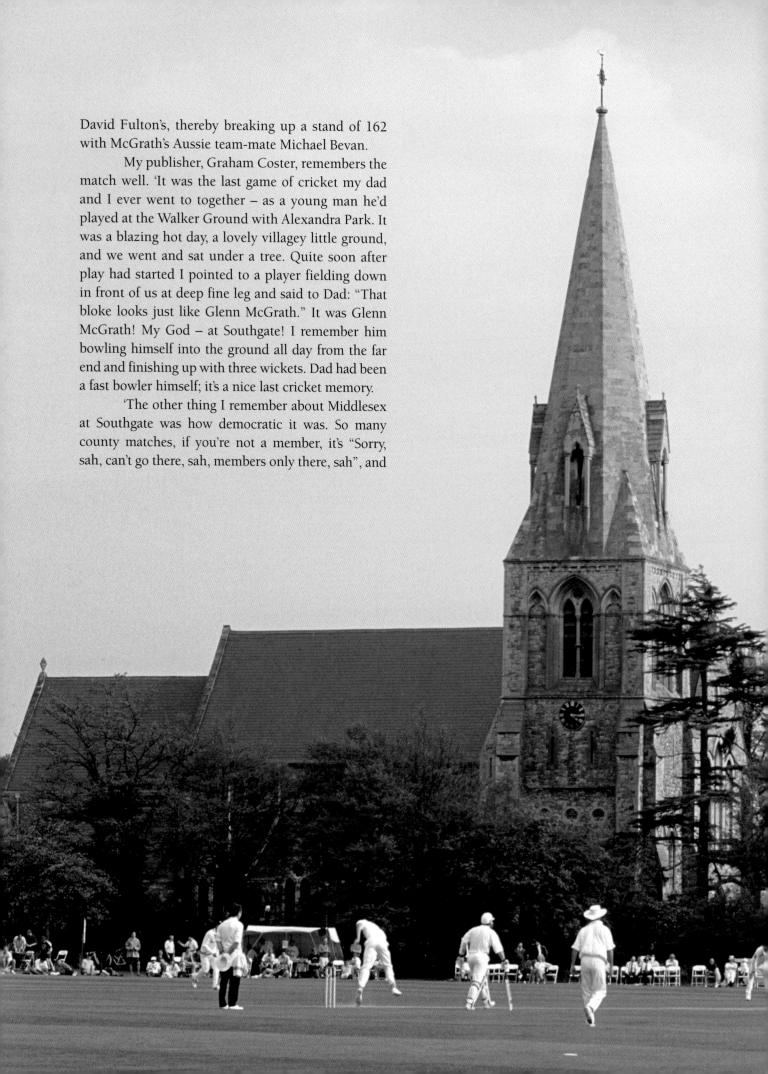

David Fulton's, thereby breaking up a stand of 162 with McGrath's Aussie team-mate Michael Bevan.

My publisher, Graham Coster, remembers the match well. 'It was the last game of cricket my dad and I ever went to together – as a young man he'd played at the Walker Ground with Alexandra Park. It was a blazing hot day, a lovely villagey little ground, and we went and sat under a tree. Quite soon after play had started I pointed to a player fielding down in front of us at deep fine leg and said to Dad: "That bloke looks just like Glenn McGrath." It was Glenn McGrath! My God – at Southgate! I remember him bowling himself into the ground all day from the far end and finishing up with three wickets. Dad had been a fast bowler himself; it's a nice last cricket memory.

'The other thing I remember about Middlesex at Southgate was how democratic it was. So many county matches, if you're not a member, it's "Sorry, sah, can't go there, sah, members only there, sah", and

▲ Previous page top:
Wellingborough School ground overlooked by its distinctivel, thatched pavilion.

▲ Previous page bottom:
Nigel Felton making runs at Wellingborough, 1986.

▼ **Below:** *The Grace Step.*

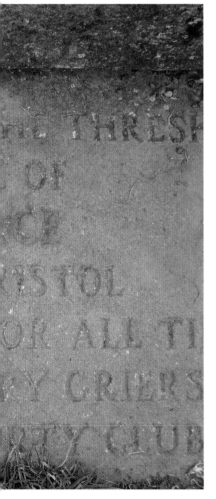

weathercock that was found among the ruins, restored and remounted. Formally relaid was W.G. Grace's former front doorstep, originally acquired for the school in 1939 by a cricket-mad geography teacher known as E. Murray Witham. He drove to Bristol in the dead of night after hearing that the house of the cricketing colossus of the Golden Age was about to be demolished. The step is inscribed with the words 'not for an age, but of all time' and superstition has it that a batsman who fails to plant a foot firmly on the stone on the way out will fail to score any runs.

Murray Witham, incidentally, used to grow his own tobacco and hang it out to dry in the pavilion's cellar. A piece was found by Harry Neal, head groundsman from 1983 to 1995, and donated to the school archives. There was a man steeped in cricketing tradition. Another groundsman might have used the tobacco for a roll-up or two. As it turned out, it was Harry's ashes that were scattered on the wicket after his death in 1997.

Northamptonshire had made their final visit six years earlier. They had been coming almost every year since 1946, playing forty-three first-class games and, from 1970 onwards, seventeen one-day games. It's a wonder the wicket held up so well, considering what was underneath it. Here I quote from the School's History:

> *From 1951 to 1965, the Grove also hosted the mysterious 'bottle-burying ceremony', when, at Hallowe'en, several masters assembled in the tea pavilion as the chapel clock struck midnight, emptied the contents of a whisky bottle, and then buried under the square itself that same bottle containing the autographs of those who had played in the county match there that year. All being well, the fifteen bottles should still be there, along with various other items – such as the remains of F.E. Bowmen's dog and the heel of a shoe, broken off in divine retribution perhaps when a lady had the audacity to walk right across the wicket.*

Mike tells me that the splendidly eccentric Murray Witham was the instigator of these jolly japes. 'No wonder this pitch doesn't produce as many runs as it used to,' he smiles. Perhaps we should also explain that the 'tea pavilion' is not the same as the thatched pavilion. It's the squat building nearby, dating back to 1883 and dwarfed by a row of horse chestnuts in full bloom. An estate agent would describe it as 'compact'. I don't know what the old lags of the county circuit used to call it, but somehow both teams would wedge themselves in here to take tea.

Handsome and characterful as it is, the thatched pavilion is none too spacious either. Mike would be the first to concede that. 'The official reason for the county's withdrawal,' he points out, 'was that they wanted to centralise. They needed a facility that was consistent and it's important to modern players to have decent changing conditions. Let's face it, the conditions here were pretty basic.'

For spectators as well as players, we might add. On the way here from the station, Maureen Coles of the Northamptonshire County Cricket Supporters' Club told me about the ladies' toilets. 'They were a big hole in the ground with some sacking round,' she recalled with a shudder.

But what about the older players: what did they feel about playing in such a setting with a thatched pavilion?

'It depends who you talk to,' says Mike. 'Ray Illingworth used to stomp up and down the boundary chuntering about the changing rooms. But then John Dye, a friend of mine who came to Northants from Kent in the early seventies, would tell you that the players couldn't wait to come to outgrounds such as this one. It was a way of breaking the monotony of the county circuit. I also had the privilege of meeting Frank Tyson who was instrumental in bringing an Australian schools touring side here. Like a lot of players from the older generation, he appreciated the deviations from the standard rhythms of the season and he was very nostalgic when he came back here.'

Tyson would have been in his youthful prime, almost pawing the ground on one of these shortish boundaries, when he took 7 for 46 in Derbyshire's first innings in 1956. There would have been a succession of visiting batsmen planting their feet wearily on the Grace step on the way back into the pavilion that day, and one or two would perhaps be quite relieved to be out of the way of the 'Typhoon'. (That was the only year, incidentally, when there were two county matches in one August week at Wellingbrough, Lancashire having departed shortly before Derbyshire arrived.)

Whether or not Len Hutton paid his respects to the doorstep on the way out to bat here in 1949 is not recorded. All we know is that he scored 269 not out for Yorkshire. Not enough, as it turned out. The match was drawn after Dennis Brookes and Norman 'Buddy' Oldfield put on 208 for the first wicket in Northamptonshire's second innings. No shortage of runs in that match. But, then, it was still two years before Murray Witham and his chums began burying Scotch bottles under the wicket.

All that crushed glass may well have had the detrimental effect. But then again there were some explosive innings here in one-day games during the seventies and eighties. Wayne Larkins and Peter Willey shared an opening stand of 202 for the first wicket against Leicestershire in 1979 and Ian Botham smashed a breathtaking 175 not out for Somerset in twenty-seven overs in 1986. A large and expectant crowd, many of them on the edge of fold-up chairs supplied by the local council, had turned up and 'Beefy' duly delivered.

Maureen was here as usual, selling club shirts and souvenirs from a marquee at long-off. She needn't have worried about a ball landing on the roof. Sixes

sailed over it. There were thirteen in all and only twelve fours. 'One six went almost to what we call "conker island",' says Mike, pointing to another row of horse chestnuts on a distant horizon, well beyond some tennis courts that have appeared since county matches ceased. 'Another went thataway, clearing the road and landing on a roof in that industrial estate,' he adds, gesturing in the other direction.

Wellingborough had seen nothing like it since Majid Khan had belted 75 in twenty-seven minutes

while playing for Glamorgan in the Sunday League.

Northamptonshire loyalists may prefer to recall a three-day match two years later when Bishen Bedi bade farewell with 5 for 24 and 6 for 83 as Middlesex were beaten by 128 runs. Certainly those old enough to remember will prefer that memory to what befell Northamptonshire on their last first-class game at the school. They lost by an innings and one run and were bowled out for 68 in a second innings in which Nottinghamshire's Franklyn Stephenson took 5 for 27 to follow up his 5 for 68 in the first.

Northamptonshire's Malachy Loye, better known as Mal and now cricket coach at Wellingborough, remembers it well. Not that he played in the match. 'I was only seventeen at the time,' he tells me while taking a brief break from the nets. But I saw it on television and it was obvious that nobody could pick the ball up from the trees beyond the sightscreen. Stephenson was not only tall; he had a slower ball that came out of the back of his hand and he made the whole of the Northants batting line-up look like idiots.' Even Allan Lamb, it would seem, who was caught Pick bowled Stephenson for two.

'The following week,' Mal goes on, 'I turned out for the second XI here against Somerset. A bloke with big ears came steaming in from the same end as Stephenson with a run-up like Richard Hadlee. "Who's this here?" we thought.'

They soon found out. Andy Caddick finished with 5 for 36 in the first innings and 6 for 36 in the second as Somerset went on to win by a wicket. Did he get you out, Mal?

'Probably. You'd better check.'

I did. M.S. Loye bowled Caddick 11 in the first innings, bowled Caddick 4 in the second.

There were evidently times when you could plant both feet on the Grace step and it made no difference whatsoever.

Left: *Players from Northamptonshire (left) and Worcestershire outside the distinctive Wellingborough School pavilion mark a minute's silence for umpire Syd Buller who had died the previous day.*

NOTTINGHAMSHIRE

~

THE TOWN GROUND, WORKSOP

Brian Clough loved cricket. As luck would have it, his office at Nottingham Forest's City Ground was just across the road from Trent Bridge – ideal for spending an hour or two relaxing in that brief period between the end of one football season and the beginning of the next. If he wanted to watch his mate Geoffrey Boycott batting for Yorkshire against Nottinghamshire, however, he usually had to up sticks and travel thirty-five miles north to Worksop.

Notts rarely strayed from their imposing and historically resonant Test ground but, when they did, Worksop was the venue more often than not. The Town Ground hosted forty-seven first-class matches and three List A games between 1921 and 1998. Yorkshire were the visitors on fourteen of those occasions. Well, the county boundary was just up the road and Sheffield is fifteen miles closer than Nottingham. Cross-border clashes on the greensward of Worksop became something of a tradition during the seventies and early eighties. The fixture tended to take place in July to coincide with the annual holidays of the collieries that abounded in north Notts and South Yorkshire.

Miners would make up a fair proportion of the crowds that piled in from the bus station on the other side of Central Avenue – until 1986 at least when relations between the two coalfields had become strained, to put it mildly, and the long-planned programme of pit closures was well underway.

It seems unlikely that Cloughie came by bus. Nor did he mingle with the sizeable Geoffrey Boycott supporters' club, or indeed seek a prime seat in the pavilion. 'He used to sit with his back to the old football stand, near to the beer tent,' says Worksop CC trustee, former chairman and first-XI captain Neil Probert. 'Sometimes he'd be on his own and sometimes with a bloke who'd go and fetch him a Scotch every now and then. He tended to disappear when Boycott was out.'

Still, he must have been detained at the Town Ground for lengthy periods. Yorkshire's tenacious opener averaged 93.1 here. In 1983 he accumulated 214 not out on a wicket that evidently suited him. That score was only surpassed in 1996 by Steve James, who hit 235 for Glamorgan in the first innings and was out for a duck in the second.

As a man of Nottinghamshire, Neil prefers to remember 1986 when the 'home' side won by an innings and the top three of Chris Broad, Tim Robinson and Paul Johnson all hit centuries. Or 1978, when Notts won by eight wickets and Sir

(as he then wasn't) Richard Hadlee turned in figures of 6 for 39 in Yorkshire's first innings of 93. 'He was running up the slope from the river end as well,' he recalls, conjuring the image of Sir Richard's run-up, memorably described by John Arlott as 'like Groucho Marx chasing a pretty waitress'.

Fred Trueman, apparently, was adamant that he was 'never going to bowl up that bloody slope'. He came steaming in from the canal end instead – to great effect in 1962 when he took 8 for 84 and reduced Notts to 126 in their first innings.

With the Chesterfield Canal at one end and the River Ryton (not quite as majestic as the Trent) at the other, it was not unknown for the ball to disappear with a splash on occasions. But Viv Richards, later Sir Vivian, bypassed the water with ease when Andy Afford tossed up one of his slow left-armers. The ball went over the trees, over the canal, over the railway line and seemed to be heading for Yorkshire. Neil takes up the story: 'We rushed out to the beer tent when we saw Viv explode into that shot and the ball was still travelling. Eventually it hit the side of the Carlton bicycle factory. It was the biggest hit I've ever seen. Massive.'

Surprise, surprise, the cycle factory is no longer there. The canal and the river *are*, of course, the latter bridged by the entrance to the Town Ground where a tree in full blossom stands sentry. It's a glorious Tuesday in early June, but it would be pushing it a bit to say that the ground looks a picture. Maybe that's because we've just come from the idyllic, tucked-away cricket field at Shireoaks, a few miles away (see p126). Or maybe it's because Worksop FC now play elsewhere and the football stand has been replaced by an extensive white wall forming the side of a branch of Wilkinson's.

The football stand at Worksop that Brian Clough sat with his back to.

Advertisements for local companies cover much of the equally faceless frontage of the squash club opposite. To the left is the clubhouse and to the right a single-storey red-brick pavilion built in the 1980s to replace the old wooden building that Larwood and Voce, Trueman and Close would have remembered. 'The old one was bigger and had more character, but it needed a lot of money spent on it,' Neil explains as we step inside and pass the time of day with the mother-in-law of the current first-XI captain. She's cleaning the kitchen to within an inch of its life.

The pavilion walls are covered in evocative photographs. We home in on a framed display with yet another cricketing knight as its centrepiece. For my money, Sir Garfield Sobers was an even finer all-rounder than Sir Richard Hadlee, Sir Ian Botham or the not-so-plain old Imran Khan. And, lest we forget, Sobers played for Nottinghamshire from 1968 to 1974. In 1971 he scored a characteristically flamboyant 78 against Middlesex here before being run out. He also finished with figures of 4 for 21 in the visitors' second innings.

Among the pictures ranged around the great man is one of David Gower bowling. Left-handed and with effortless style, of course. In fact, he's playing crown-green bowls round the back of the pavilion on a rain-interrupted day. Looking on is his Leicestershire team-mate Phil de Freitas, as well as Chris Broad and Paul Johnson.

There are more photos in the bar of the nearby clubhouse, including one of Trueman with his pal Jack Baddiley, who was president of Notts for some years. 'They always had a drink together after the day's play,' Neil recalls, 'and Fred used to stay at Jack's farmhouse.' That was quite nearby. Baddiley was a Worksop man and it seems likely that his influence kept the county coming to the Town Ground for as long as they did. After his death in 1991, the visits became less frequent. There were none at all between 1992 and 1996. 'By the time the fixture list had been reduced and they told us there wouldn't be enough matches to let Worksop have a game,' Neil goes on. 'But then there were a couple of times when Trent Bridge was needed for extra

matches on the international scene and they came back for three games in the late nineties. They were four-day games by that time and the last two, against Essex and Leicestershire, both went right down to the final session.'

Which suggests that the wicket was holding up well. Not that it would ever be as good as the one at Trent Bridge, needless to say. A few days before setting off for Worksop I'd called in at the grand old ground for a chat with Peter Wynne-Thomas, the county's distinguished historian and statistician. Peter's lair in the library hadn't change much since I was last here two years ago. In fact, it probably hasn't changed for decades. In here it could be the 1970s, the 1960s, the 1950s or earlier. You wouldn't be surprised if he answered the phone and calmly informed you that Reg Simpson or Joe Hardstaff had just reached his century.

Sporting a natty pair of braces, Peter was sitting at his manual typewriter at the far end of an enormous table strewn with papers and books. Many more books were crammed into the shelves

Above: *Geoff Boycott whose average at Worksop was over 93.*

◀ **Left:** *The Town Ground on a rather gloomy day.*

with well-weathered files wedged in around them. Images of William Clarke, George Parr and other Trent Bridge legends peered down from high above them.

As I expected, Peter had not only visited all the county's outgrounds, he had also typed up notes about them with little diagrams at the bottom. So I learnt that the boundaries at the Town Ground were 136 yards across and 131 yards the other way, 'only slightly smaller than Trent Bridge'; that Notts played eleven first-class matches at Elm Avenue, Newark, where Derek Randall made 78 on his debut in 1972, including a six into the adjacent cemetery; that Nottinghamshire ventured over the Lincolnshire border to play a couple of first-class matches in the flatlands of Cleethorpes in the 1980s and a few more List A games in the nineties and noughties. They also entertained Sri Lanka there twice, in 1984 and 1990.

'The Cleethorpes club made a tremendous effort to make us welcome,' Peter recalled. 'There were marquees all round the ground. But the Sri Lankans weren't too happy. Like most players of the modern era, they like their home comforts and wanted to be at Trent Bridge.'

Having bid farewell, I walked back over the said bridge towards the city centre. To the right I could see the Brian Clough Stand at the City Ground. I was living in Nottingham in the seventies when he arrived with his 'oppo', Peter Taylor, and they transformed Forest from a Second Division outfit into League champions before going on to land the European Cup and then retain it the following year. As far as the fans were concerned, Clough could walk over the Trent without a bridge.

But I also liked the idea that he would sometimes walk across the road to watch cricket and that a man with such a short fuse had the patience to wait while Boycott assembled a century with assiduous care. Not surprisingly, Geoffrey liked the idea, too. When Clough died in 2004, he wrote a generous tribute in the *Daily Telegraph*, describing him as 'an absolute jewel, a diamond and a true friend' who 'loved his cricket, understood it and came to see me bat whenever he had the chance at Middlesbrough, Scarborough and Worksop.'

STEETLEY COMPANY GROUND, SHIREOAKS

We drive past a handsomely restored row of former miners' cottages, turn sharp left at a Victorian pump house with hanging baskets adorning its mellow red brick. Cow parsley froths and surges from the verges as Neil Probert's Citröen cruises down a narrow lane.

Two Roy Harper songs spring to mind. Well, Neil is an old cricketer who long ago left the crease (see above) and it's one of those days in England. The sun's shining, June is busting out all over (where do these songs keep coming from?) and we're on our way to see a little piece of cricketing history.

The expressions 'picturesque' and 'former mining village' rarely go together, but that's the case here in the heart of Shireoaks, surely the most obscure place ever to stage first-class cricket. Only one match, mind you, and that was back in 1961. It was so obscure that *Wisden* recorded it as talking place in Worksop, a couple of miles up the road.

The ground used to be owned by the Steetley Company, manufacturers of foundry bricks. Managing director Wilf Stocks had a passion for cricket. He

▼ **Below and right:** *Shireoaks still in use for club cricket.*

also had a dream. And that dream came true when Sussex turned up to play Nottinghamshire on a July day over fifty years ago. No mean player himself, Wilf scored 52 in 1935 when he opened the batting for Shireoaks in their famous victory over a Worksop side that boasted five county players.

By 1950 he was in full control of the company and spared no expense in creating his own works ground. There were six ground staff alone. 'Recruitment policy discriminated in favour of the best local cricketers,' Stephen Chalke points out in *The Way It Was*. Wilf's cousin Freddie Stocks became a sales rep and Eric Martin was transport manager.

Perhaps they still had some influence at Trent Bridge by the early sixties because at least twenty-two county players, a couple of umpires and some intrepid members found their way here. As the Notts off-spinner Bomber Wells told Stephen: 'The wicket was superb, but it was in the middle of nowhere. I remember Jim Parks saying: "The best way of getting us here would have been to have us parachuted in."'

Alan Oakman was glad he made the trip. He hit 229 for Sussex, the second double century of the match. The first was scored by Norman Hill for Notts who finished on 201 not out, only to see his side lose by nine wickets. 'He was a good lad, Norman, except that he talked all the time,' Alan told me from his home in Edgbaston, Birmingham. 'As for me, it was the only double century I ever got. I remember poor old Richard Langridge [his opening partner] being very unlucky. He was run out [for 11] by a direct hit and the fielder only had one stump to aim at. Can't remember who it was.'

The runs never flowed as sweetly again for A.S.M. Oakman. No wonder that whenever the annual away fixture against Notts came around he

would plead: 'Why can't we go back to Steetley?'

If he went back now, he would find that surprisingly little has changed. Neil's Citroën comes to a halt at a dead end. Ahead is a five-bar gate leading to open countryside and a fishing club's lake. To the right is a whitewashed garden gate through which we pass into what proves to be an enchanted garden for any lover of cricket. Once we've strolled up the drive, the field is revealed in what looks to me like rustic splendour. Neil, though, is looking disapprovingly at one or two daisies in the outfield. 'It used to be immaculate,' he says as one whose club playing career spanned two generations of Nottinghamshire

cricketers. He played against Freddie Stocks in the early sixties – 'they were always a tremendous team, Shireoaks, because of the Steetley connection' – and with Tim Robinson in the seventies when they opened the batting together for Worksop before Robinson went on to bigger things.

The ground is encircled by mature trees and, in one case, a spreading bush that has obscured the frontage of the ancient scoreboard, now past its 'score-by' date. A huge horse chestnut, decked out in early summer finery, towers over the substantial hut where the Steetley ground staff used to keep all their equipment. There are some white benches in front that once offered a view behind the bowler's arm. 'But they've turned the wicket,' Neil notes, 'from east-west to north-south.'

The 'hut' is now the pavilion used by Woodsetts, who play in division four of the Bassetlaw League. 'It serves its purpose,' medium-pace bowler Jonathan Steeple tells me. 'Eventually we hope to build a new one.'

The original red-brick pavilion is now a private house, and a very handsome one, too, with a balcony and a clock tower. It's owned by a local doctor. But perhaps we should raise a glass to one John Small and his wife who acquired the property and the adjoining land back in the nineties from the American company that had bought Steetley without realising that they'd also bought a cricket ground. For years it lay unused. Luckily, green-belt laws prevented anyone building houses on the land where Oakman and Hill once stroked their double tons. The Smalls, bless 'em, made their home in the pavilion, restored the clock, brought back the old groundsman and cricket resumed.

'We're now trying to buy the land from Mr Small, who's moved to Spain,' Jonathan confides. 'Eventually we're hoping the Shireoaks team will return here and play on Sundays.'

If that sounds like a fanciful dream, remember the story of the Stocks of Steetley: Wilf and Freddie. Dreams sometimes come true.

SOMERSET

~

RECREATION GROUND, BATH

The gateway to that part of the Recreation Ground once devoted to first-class cricket is flanked by two turnstiles that look from a distance like upmarket Parisian *pissoirs*. Close up they are a lot more fragrant as well as displaying an architectural *je ne sais quoi* that seems to say that this may not be Paris but it is Bath and therefore a bit special.

It's easy to imagine that a festival here would have been very special indeed. To enjoy the full visual effect, admittedly, you'd have to sit with your back to one of the few blots on the landscape. The rear end of the sports and leisure centre, somehow given planning permission in the early 1970s, looks like a multi-storey car park. But looking out from it you can see, to the right, the lush green hills where I spent a night in a sleeping bag under the stars on the eve of England's World Cup triumph in 1966. (I was seventeen, naïve and freezing.) To the left, Bath Abbey peers loftily over the Wadworth 6X Stand of Bath Rugby Club and the cry of gulls from the river between resonates across the wide-open spaces.

Towers, turrets and spires are much in evidence elsewhere on the horizon. Any batsman offering up a prayer as Fred Rumsey prepared to run in on a wicket that the venerable cricket writer David Frith describes as 'always capricious' had no shortage of religious buildings to provide reassurance. We'll get back to the wicket in a moment. First let's complete the scene by noting the elegant four- and five-storey town houses in Bath stone, largely screened from view by beeches and birches, two of which were planted by Greg Chappell and Brian Close before Somerset pulled off a seven-wicket victory against the Australians in 1977.

The trees tower over the pavilion, built in 1897, the same year that Somerset welcomed the 'Gentlemen of Philadelphia'. With its red pantiled rood, this listed building would have been in its infancy when Warwick Armstrong's Australian 'Invincibles' were held to an unlikely draw by the county side in 1903, despite 303 from Armstrong himself. It would have been in its prime in 1919 when Jack 'Farmer' White took 16 Worcestershire wickets for 83; not to mention 1923 when Jack Hobbs scored his hundredth hundred here. But it would have been showing its age by 1985 when Vic Marks took 8 for 17 in 22 overs (15 of them maidens) to skittle Lancashire for 89.

Today the pavilion looks much better from a distance than it does close up. Peeling paintwork is all too evident, while one of the windows is cracked and

The Recreation Ground in the Golden Age.

smeared with bird dung. Peering through a more transparent pane confirms that the facilities are nowhere near the standard expected by today's first-class cricketers. Even those players who plied their trade in the 1960s and 1970s were not overly impressed. Slow left-armer Peter Robinson was one of the old pros who enjoyed the festival circuit on the whole but, when I ask him about the Recreation Ground's pavilion, he responds wryly: 'It was okay apart from the green stains around the bath and the splinters in the floor. I remember Brian Close getting the groundsman to hammer in some six-inch nails so that he could hang his clothes up.'

What about the surroundings, though, Peter? Some setting, eh?

'Yes, it all looked very nice with the marquees and everything. Mind you, the pitch might as well have been at Dunkirk. I remember my first appearance at Bath in 1965 against my former county, Worcestershire. Cecil Bottle, the Somerset groundsman, came up from Taunton, took one look at the wicket and flooded it with marl. The result was that it came out like dinner plates. Basil D'Oliveira got one of the best noughts that you've ever seen in the first innings and they were bowled out for 42 in the second. Rumsey did the damage. I didn't do much.'

You didn't do so badly the following year, I point out: 7 for 48 in Surrey's first innings.

'They'd tried to improve the wicket by bringing in a groundsman from Lansdown Cricket Club, who also worked for the AA. I told him he might as well put some loose chippings down and some signs up saying "Please drive carefully". Mickey Stewart bagged a pair and the ball turned square.'

It must have been a bit like that in 1953 when poor old Bertie Buse scuppered the takings from his own benefit match by taking 6 Lancashire wickets for 41, thereby helping to ensure that the game was over on the first day after Somerset were bowled out for 55 and 79. At that time a festival at Bath was supposed to last for ten days – three three-day matches with a Sunday off in between. The groundsman's response to the one-day debacle of 1953 was to roll bull's blood from a nearby abattoir into the pitch. Somerset's response was to win the next game against Kent and lose the following one against Leicestershire. In the course of those two matches, Brian Langford took 25 wickets for 290 runs, having bought some new boots with a few shillings given to him by the Somerset secretary, one Air Vice-Marshal Taylor. Aged just seventeen, Langford found himself propelled to the top of the national bowling averages ahead of Alec Bedser.

Sixty years on and, although I'm no Michael Atherton or Mark Nicholas, the wicket looks pretty good to me – flattish and biscuit-coloured. The hot, dry weather has obviously helped. 'I've had a lot of compliments about it,' current groundsman David Cobb confides. Not from Somerset, however, who haven't played a first-class match here since 2006, and not even from Bath Cricket Club, which plays at a much smaller ground across the road. Pub teams now use the county first-class strip where, lest we forget, class batsmen have made high scores irrespective of the wicket's capriciousness. Indeed Zaheer Abbas hit 215 not out and 150 not out for neighbouring Gloucestershire here in 1981.

It won't surprise you to learn that Somerset's reduction of and final withdrawal from first-class matches at Bath was primarily for financial reasons.

At one time this was a county almost as itinerant as Essex. They played at Weston-super-Mare and Frome (see pages 134 and 138) as well as Yeovil, where Langford once bowled eight successive maidens in a Sunday League match, Wells,

The Recreation Ground provided a stunning setting for county cricket, as long as the leisure centre was behind you.

Glastonbury, Millfield School and various parts of Bristol. Oh yes, and Torquay in Devon. 'But in recent times some £6 million has been spent on upgrading Taunton,' says Michael Davis MBE, chairman of the Bath and Wiltshire Area of Somerset CCC. As a former finance director of a public company, he can well understand that they need to maximise their income in the south of the county. 'But we can get to Lord's quicker than we can get to Taunton,' he points out. It is, after all, a distance of nearly seventy-two miles from Bath. Bear in mind that old pros such as Peter Robinson used to have to drive there and back every day for nine days at festival time. 'After close of play, we'd nip across the road and have a pint with the opposition,' Peter recalls. 'But we wouldn't have another one until we reached the George and Pilgrims in Glastonbury. It helped to break up the journey home.'

Players in more recent times would expect to be put up in a hotel in Bath, adding to the considerable cost of playing in the north of the county. 'It cost around £80,000 to set up a festival here and when Richard Gould arrived from Bristol City as chief executive in 2005 he decided that it was too risky,' Michael goes on. 'Instead we were granted a one-day game, cutting the costs to £25,000.'

He's telling me this while we take shelter from the midday sun in one of the covered stands at the rugby club. Quite appropriate in the circumstances. In 2009, Mr Gould floated the idea of playing cricket on the rugby pitch. It would be a joint venture with Bath RFC, who would share the costs, provide decent changing facilities for the players and corporate hospitality from their boxes. The chief executive accepted an offer to move to Surrey shortly before the one-day game had been reduced to a Twenty20 match against Essex in 2011.

'Eight thousand people turned up, and that was for a fag-end fixture against Essex on a Monday night,' says Michael as if to demonstrate his point that 'Somerset CCC are still committed in principle to playing at Bath because it's a honey-pot'.

That may be so, but they haven't visited for the past two years, I point out. 'Well, in 2012 it never stopped raining and we couldn't get the outfield ready in time, so they switched the game to Taunton. The same happened in 2013 because an ECB inspector came down from Lord's in March and didn't like the look of the wicket.'

From my admittedly non-expert point of

view, it didn't look much better in mid-July. Nor did that part of the outfield where the temporary East Stand of the rugby ground comes down between April and August. Bath RFC have long had plans to expand and Michael, a glass-half-full-man if ever I've met one, sees all sorts of opportunities for Somerset to make use of the ground during future summers. That may prove to be the case but, at time of writing, planning permission has yet to be granted.

What we can probably assume for the foreseeable future is that the county will not return to the site of so many memorable festivals on the field to our right. Diana Gibney, a longstanding Bath and Wilts member who is sitting with us in the rugby stand, has fond memories that will stay with her while the wrangling over the Recreation Ground goes on. Of Ian Botham hitting 55 in 28 balls and scattering the picnickers on the green mound next to the pavilion. Of meeting people from all over

north-east Somerset and Wiltshire she hadn't seen since the previous festival. Of an almost village fête atmosphere behind the temporary stands and the fold-up seats. 'There was a guess-the-weight of the cake competition and a tombola run by a lovely man called Ted Lewis,' she says. 'He died earlier this year at ninety-eight. Went to his first festival in 1924.'

That would have been the year after Hobbs's hundredth hundred and the pavilion would have been in its youthful prime. Alas, the first match of three was abandoned without a ball being bowled. But in the second H.S.R (Humphrey Seymour Ramsay) Critchley-Salmonson returned to Somerset after a dozen years playing cricket in Argentina and took 4 for 60 in Derbyshire's second innings to help the hosts to a 192-run victory. In the following match, Critchley-Salmonson contributed 66 to what was then Somerset's highest total of 675 for 9 declared in response to Hampshire's 453. That capricious wicket was obviously behaving itself. The turnstiles inside those Parisian *pissoir* gateways to the ground would have been clicking away merrily and, with that neo-brutalist sports and leisure centre still some way in the future, the setting would have been unforgettable.

▲ **Above:** *A.G. Bajana behind a marquee at Bath.*

◀ **Left:** *The days when Bath Abbey was not obscured by the Wadworths's 6X stand.*

CLARENCE PARK, WESTON-SUPER-MARE

Let's stay focused for a moment on Humphrey Seymour Ramsay Critchley-Salmonson, who we left making his comeback for Somerset at Bath (see above) after twelve years in South America. That name is so redolent of the world of pre-war English 'Gentlemen' cricketers, containing as it does so many syllables – nine more than plain old Jack Hobbs, a 'Player' with considerably more talent who gained another syllable when he was knighted. Having scored a few runs and taken a few wickets at the Recreation Ground in June 1924, Critchley-Salmonson popped up at the Weston-super-Mare festival the following month and helped to beat Sussex by an innings and 162 runs, turning in figures of 5 for 23 in the first innings and 2 for 21 in the second.

Fair play to good old HSR, then. The sea air evidently suited him and, indeed, the other Somerset players of the day. Jack White was particularly fond of Clarence Park. 'Lovely' was how he described it while strongly resisting talk of moving the festival away in 1936. His team-mate R.C. Robertson-Glasgow, who had more of a way with words, described the Weston festival as 'a thing of marquees where the right stuff could be found, and deckchairs and wooden chairs under which the spade and bucket could be packed for an hour or two'.

As it turned out, Somerset did not stop coming in 1936. They waited another sixty years. It was in 1996 that the last first-class and, indeed, one-day game was played here, against Durham. In its heyday the festival hosted three consecutive

three-day games.

Somerset started coming in 1914, only to have their visits rudely interrupted by the First World War. They didn't return again until 1919. The park itself had been donated to the town by one Rebecca Davies in 1882. Exactly a century later, Simon Hughes arrived as part of the successful Middlesex side of the 1980s. He was not exactly enamoured with the place.

'Weston was the quintessential county cricket venue,' wrote the man from Lord's in *A Lot of Hard Yakka*. 'It had a sloping wicket, a bumpy outfield (which for most of the year was a public dog toilet), marquees, deckchairs, temporary stands and the constant hum of generators powering beer pumps and ice-cream vans. And the world's smallest pavilion, actually an enlarged park-keeper's hut, but barely adequate to keep chickens in. The dressing rooms were full of shrapnel-sized splinters, but it didn't matter: once everyone had wedged their cricket cases in there was no floor space visible anyway.'

The pavilion is still there, looking 'compact', as an estate agent might put it. Anti-graffiti paint appears to have done little to deter vandals from covering it with their handiwork in parts as well as bodging the odd hole here and there. The dog-walkers are still there, too, in some numbers. Well, it is a green, wide-open space in a pleasant residential area. We can see substantial Victorian and Edwardian villas through trees that are in full leaf and apparently remain so throughout the year. Clarence Park is well known locally not only for its pines but also its South African oaks. They look very similar to English oaks, but I'm reliably informed that their leaves linger longer.

While his pooch pees up a tree, a sprightly septuagenarian tells me that he sat at the far side of the ground with a bottle of lemonade as a boy watching Michael Walford compiling '250-odd' for Somerset against Hampshire in 1947. It was 264, to be precise. M.M. Walford, a triple blue at Oxford who would go on to represent his country at hockey in the 1948 Olympics, was another of those amateurs whose performances were time-limited. As a master at Sherborne School, Dorset, he could only turn out

At Clarence Park cricket festivals had to assembled from scratch.

for the county in the summer holidays.

Weston's cricket festival was almost invariably staged in August, the height of the holiday season. 'It was nice to play by the sea if the weather was fine,' Peter Robinson recalls. 'You never knew who was going to turn up. When we played Glamorgan, the Welsh supporters used to come up the Bristol Channel by paddle steamer.'

Like Simon Hughes, he remembers the splinters in the pavilion floor but, unlike Hughes, he didn't have Lord's to go home to. 'Facilities at the county ground [Taunton] weren't much better than

Clarence Park in my day,' he says. His day was the 1960s and 1970s. Taunton is much improved today and, having spent £6 million on upgrades, the county is far less inclined to up sticks and play elsewhere.

Peter Anderson was the Somerset chief executive who decided to forgo the annual trip to Weston. By that time, County Championship matches were played over four rather than three days and the number of fixtures had been reduced. The cost could no longer be justified.

The sheer scale of the operation can be gleaned from a conversation I had with Chris

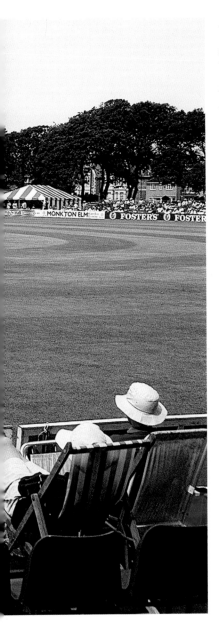

▲ **Above:** *South African oaks still encircle Clarence Park.*

Webber, who was born two roads away from the pitch and grew up to be parks superintendent. 'My main responsibilities were on the floral side,' he emphasises. He was responsible for the dazzling flower beds that required cricket lovers almost to don their sun glasses before passing through that part of the park across the road from the cricket ground, en route to the nearby sea front during the lunch interval. There are still some impressive blooms today, but nothing like on the same scale. 'We had sixty staff in those days,' says Chris. 'Today it's about twenty-five.'

His own involvement with the festival started early. 'My uncle was catering manager for what used to be called the Weston Corporation, and he'd give me a box filled with dry ice and Wall's briquettes to take around the festival crowds. I was thirteen or fourteen at the time [the late sixties] and a bit self-conscious. But I sold a fair few on hot days.'

A fair few pints went down as well. 'The beer tent ran all the way down that side,' he explains, pointing towards those South African oaks to the left of the pavilion. 'Some members of the Parks Department, who were Somerset members, would take a couple of weeks off, don their blazers and spend a lot of time in that tent.'

They probably felt that they'd earned it after spending a month beforehand erecting stands and marquees to create a festive atmosphere for holidaymakers and cricket aficionados. The wicket had to be mowed, rolled and watered when necessary; the outfield kept as free as possible of bumps, nub-ends and dog poo before two groundsmen arrived from Taunton to give it the once over.

Today you can see a faint trace of the crease and the three holes where the stumps once stood. But no cricket is played here. The local club plays elsewhere. The ground once preserved for anything from five to nine days of county cricket a season now stages occasional football matches and croquet tournaments as well as providing a space for exercising Weston's canine population.

Meanwhile, Weston's cricket lovers are left with their memories. It was here that Vic Marks scored his maiden century for Somerset in 1984 after ten years with the county; here also that Ian Botham, a Somerset smiter in the tradition of Wellard and Gimblett, kept the holidaymakers happy by bludgeoning ten sixes on his way to 134 against Northamptonshire in 1985.

He didn't do quite so well three years previously against Middlesex, however, as Simon Hughes recalls with some relish. After 'a back-foot thump which nearly took gully's head off', he tried to repeat the shot and 'got a thick edge to third slip which Gatting clung on to'. Viv Richards had fared marginally better, caught Edmonds bowled Cowans for 35. But both Somerset superstars went for ducks in the second innings as the home side slumped to 57 all out in eight overs.

That festival match was over by midday in glorious sunshine, bad news for cricket-loving holidaymakers and travelling Somerset supporters, but satisfying for the men from Lord's as they unwedged their cricket bags, picked the splinters from their feet and hit the road out of Weston.

THE AGRICULTURAL SHOWGROUNDS, FROME

These days it's known simply as the Showground, 'home of the Showmen'. Frome Cricket Club, in other words. But in the pre- and post-war years it was one of Somerset's many outgrounds and there was a certain agricultural ambience to both the surroundings and the cricket. This was a place where ruddy–faced farmers might gather to show off prize Friesian bulls or trade in rounds of Cheddar at the annual Agricultural and Cheese Show a month or two after seeing off several ciders in anticipation of Arthur Wellard bombarding the boundaries.

Wellard hit almost a quarter of his nigh-on 12,500 runs in sixes, seventy-two of them coming in one season: 1935. At Frome that year he was out (stumped) for 21 in Somerset's only innings. He did, though, take 5 for 66 in Essex's first innings.

London Mayor Sir Rowland Blades opening the ground in Kingston in 1927. Surrey played two games there after the war.

SUSSEX

THE SAFFRONS, EASTBOURNE

The drive from Brighton to Eastbourne always seems to take longer than expected. It's only twenty-four miles, but I'm stuck behind a lumbering lorry and there are very few opportunities to overtake on the largely single-track A27. Sussex players and members must have felt the same frustration when travelling to play or watch at The Saffrons or, indeed, at the Central Ground, Hastings (see page 156), which is even further beyond this long and winding road. Alan Oakman once told me that Sussex made more money on a wet day at Hove than a sunny day at Hastings because the members lived locally.

Left: Restitas Maori commun... is dulcimate is porerobus... onsed o...

the Gentlemen of the South against the Players of the South. Only a few days previously he'd belted 119 for Gloucestershire against Sussex.

There must have been something about the sea air that encouraged batsmen to throw caution to the briny breeze. Maurice Tate wrote of Cricket Week, 1935, at his favourite ground: 'Never since I have been playing for Sussex have I seen so many sixes at the Central Ground. Some were tremendous swipes.' Tate himself had been known to deposit balls into Queen's Road and cause spectators to leap from their deckchairs in the elevated gardens of Devonshire Road.

Hastings hosted a piece of cricketing history in 1947 when Denis Compton broke Sir Jack Hobbs's longstanding record by scoring his seventeenth century of the summer with the second ball after tea. And in 1975, Tony Greig smote four successive sixes off the bowling of Warwickshire off-spinner Peter Lewington.

He had scored 226 when he unadvisedly went for the fifth and was caught on the long-on boundary by Dennis Amiss.

Dennis doesn't remember taking that catch but he does recall 'John Jameson and myself getting a few runs'. Just a few – 143 for Amiss and 112 for Jameson as Warwickshire shrugged off Greig's lively double ton to win by eight wickets. Dennis had also scored 73 in the first innings. 'It was a lovely ground,' he agrees. 'And it was always nice to get away from the big Test arenas to play in such a relaxed atmosphere at such a scenic venue.'

Derek Underwood was even more enthusiastic about Hastings, and with good reason. 'It was usually a very special place for me,' he once told me, 'and I was naturally very disappointed when I heard that they were going to build on it. All my best achievements seem to have been at Hastings. I remember taking 9 for 28 against Sussex in 1964. That remains my best bowling analysis. And I got my only first-class century at the Central Ground. Must have been twenty years later.'

Spot on. A headline in the *Daily Mirror* from 3 July 1984, read: 'Deadly Derek finally gets that ton at 39'. He was finally out lbw bowled Reeve for 111. The match, incidentally, ended in a tie.

There would have been plenty of Kentish folk there to see that extraordinary game. It was far easier to get to Hastings from parts of Kent than it was to wend your way to and fro along the A27 from Brighton and Hove. Those Sussex members who made the trip to see Ted Dexter's comeback match in 1968 would not have been disappointed. He set about Underwood with some relish. By the time Deadly Derek finally got his man, Dexter had reached 203. No traffic jams on the A27 for Lord Ted, by the way. He arrived and departed by private plane.

However you travelled to cricket week at the Central Ground, by plane or train, road or boat, I hope you'll agree that the final lines of *Cricket at Hastings*, written in 1989 by Gerald Brodribb, are worth repeating:

> *The sea is near: the channel winds blow up from the west and bring the screaming gulls: they swoop on the outfield until the ball hurries them away. There is shelter in this enclosed arena with its terraced walls of houses, and the slanting sunlight shines on distant windows. High above, the ruined castle looks down on this intimate oasis of peace amid the busy town. But not for long now. I cannot be the only one who feels that the passing of this unique ground hurts like the loss of a dear friend.*

Elegant boarding houses overlooking the Central Ground.

THE MANOR GROUND, WORTHING

It wasn't just the 1931 mayor of Eastbourne who could be rude about visiting counties from 'the North'. The town clerk of Worthing was extremely dismissive of Northamptonshire, which he may well have assumed was in the North insofar as it's sited somewhere above the upper reaches of the Northern Line on the London Underground. As soon as Sussex's 1949 fixture list was published, he began complaining that the town's Manor Sports Ground had been fobbed off with second-rate opposition.

To which the Sussex secretary responded: 'With regard to Northants, somebody must have them.' W.C. Brown, the former Northants secretary who had moved to Brighton, reflected sadly: 'It did not seem in the best of taste for one county club to refer to another in much the same way as a smallpox epidemic.' But at least the story had a 'satisfying ending', as Matthew Engel and Andrew Radd report in their book *The History of Northamptonshire County Cricket Club*: 'Northamptonshire won the match very easily.'

Worthing lost its cricket festival fifteen years later, ending a tradition that had begun in 1935 and included forty-three first-class matches. The wicket might have had something to do with it. Sussex were bowled out for 23 in their second innings – almost 100 fewer than they scored in the first. The opponents were from even further north than Northamptonshire. Sussex lost by 182 runs to Warwickshire. But at least they redeemed themselves later in that week in June 1964 by beating Notts by 114 runs, largely thanks to a second-innings century from Jim Parks.

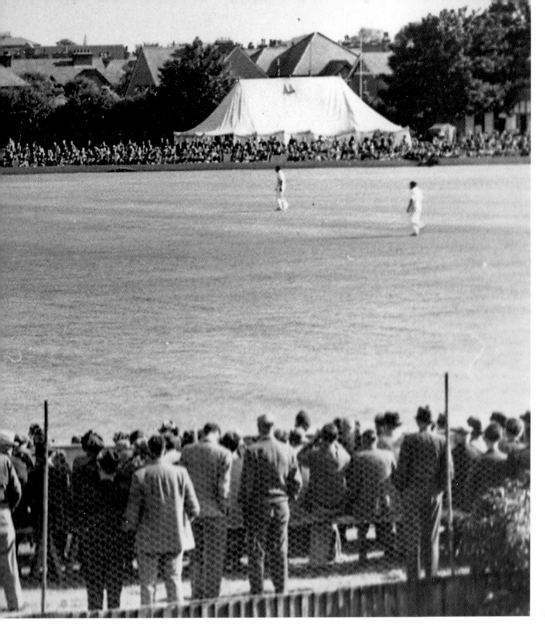

◀ **Left:** *The distinctive 1930s pavilion overlooking the Manor Ground.*

The largest crowd by far to attend a first-class match in Sussex was not at Worthing, Eastbourne, Hastings, Arundel or Horsham. Nor was it at Chichester where, despite the handsome surroundings of Priory Park, the county first XI stopped visiting in 1950. And it wasn't even at Hove.

No, Sheffield Park, Uckfield, attracted more than three times the capacity of the county's headquarters when some 25,000 turned up on the first day to watch Lord Sheffield's XI take on the Australians and win a low-scoring match by eight wickets in May 1896. The Prince of Wales was photographed pulling on his gloves outside the Ladies' Pavilion, one of two exotically ornate late Victorian structures.

W.G. Grace was there, of course. He had his beard parted by the third bouncer in an over from Ernie 'Jonah' Jones. When Grace strode down the wicket to protest, Jones muttered: 'Sorry, Doctor, she slipped.' Today 'the Arundel of Victorian England', as the late-lamented Christopher Martin-Jenkins called it, is owned by the National Trust. The hitherto itinerant Armadillos CC, largely made up of lawyers, has played there since 2009. But they will have to play there for a while yet before their aggregate attendance approaches 25,000.

WARWICKSHIRE

~

SWAN'S NEST LANE, STRATFORD-UPON-AVON
PLUS COVENTRY AND NUNEATON

Shakespeare makes no reference to cricket for obvious reasons. The Bard died some 150 years before the game evolved into something that perhaps only the English could have invented. Another two hundred years or so would pass before his home town was given the opportunity to stage a first-class match (against Oxford University). A full fifty-three years after that, Swan's Nest Lane, home of the Stratford Sports Club, was finally granted a County Championship game.

You might imagine that a few days by the banks of the Avon would be a welcome change for players and officials of Warwickshire CCC. If so, you'd be wrong. With maybe a few exceptions, players and officials are wary of the wicket and the facilities at anywhere new. As for members, they rarely like travelling and, sure enough, the distinctive sound of the Brummie whinge could be heard at Stratford during the matches against Lancashire in 2004 and Hampshire in 2005.

Let's face it: Warwickshire CCC has always appeared reluctant to leave Edgbaston. Heaven knows why. It's a great Test-match venue, to be sure. But as one who spent part of his school summer holidays there at a time when county cricket was more popular than it is today, I can confirm that a weekday Championship match generates about as much atmosphere as one of those huge Birmingham road-house pubs after the surrounding factories closed down.

Industry provided the backdrop to Warwickshire's outgrounds in the past. Mining, too, in the case of Griff and Coton, Nuneaton, which hosted twenty-six first-class matches between 1930 and 1989. The ground was once overlooked by the winding gear of a local pit and a colliery band used to strike up when the county came to town. My boyhood hero, Tom Cartwright, hit a double hundred there against Middlesex in 1962. Two years later he took 4 for 3 and 5 for 37 as Nottinghamshire were dismissed for 34 in the first innings and 57 in the second.

Cartwright was even more in his element when they sent him back to his home city of Coventry where he had worked for a while on the track at Humber, one of many car factories in the vicinity with tiptop sporting facilities. Morris Motors staged two first-class games in 1931 and 1932. But, as the thirties wore on, it was a textile manufacturer that developed the grandest ground in the city: it was Courtaulds that Warwickshire would grace with its presence, at least once and usually twice a season between 1949 and 1982; Courtaulds, with its

*The Bard's burial place
overlooking the Swan's Nest.*

Imposing pavilion and crowds that were 'sizeable and appreciative', as Dennis Amiss once told me; Courtaulds, where dashing batsmen such as Rohan Kanhai and Barry Richards gorged themselves on comparatively short boundaries; Courtaulds, where Brian Statham took fifteen wickets for Lancashire in 1957; Courtaulds, where Cartwright helped himself to 8 Hampshire wickets for 45 in 1963.

For a local lad that must have been quite something. As he told his biographer Stephen Chalke, he used to watch county matches there as a boy: 'You could see everything about the fielders; they almost trod on you. In the intervals we'd play cricket with a bottle and a tennis ball. And at 5.30 people from all the car factories would come down the path between the works and the pavilion and stand seven or eight deep, watching.'

The pavilion, built at what had seemed an immense cost of £15,000 in 1935, was somewhat the worse for wear by 1982 when Middlesex turned up for what turned out to be the last first-class match. Their pace bowler Simon Hughes was not impressed. 'The pavilion was ramshackle and full of what appeared to be the former contents of a church hall,' he writes in

A Lot of Hard Yakka, his account of a county cricketer's life. 'The jumble of furniture left very little room for manoeuvre and when I pulled a muscle in my back the only area for the physio to treat me lying down was underneath a grand piano. Honestly.'

Hughes was used to rather less cluttered surroundings. He played most of his home games at Lord's. Gladstone Small, meanwhile, was used to Edgbaston, but that doesn't explain why the future England bowler sent down eleven no-balls in one over of the Middlesex game. He must have been happier than most to say farewell to Courtaulds.

Well, the ground has long been a wasteland and the factory, a shadow of its former self, finally closed in 2007. The county played three matches at Coventry and North Warwickshire's Bull's Head ground in the early nineties, Allan Donald seeming to start his run-up out on the Binley Road and Mike Gatting hitting brisk centuries for Middlesex in both innings in 1992. But only the Warwickshire second team plays there these days. After that heavy loss to Middlesex, the first XI retreated to Edgbaston and played its home games there for the next twelve years.

In the post-industrial twenty-first-century

The River Avon beyond six-hitting distance.

it seems somehow appropriate that they were finally tempted away to a town that has thrived on marketing itself as the birthplace of a man who spun words more sublimely than Courtaulds could ever spin fibres. Even then there was a big dose of expediency behind the exercise, as *Birmingham Mail* cricket correspondent Brian Halford points out in his book *The Year of the Bear*, the story of Warwickshire's 2004 Championship triumph. Edgbaston was to be one of the three host grounds for the lucrative ICC Championship Trophy and groundsman Steve Rouse needed some time to work on the square.

But they might not necessarily have chosen Stratford had not club chairman Paul Biddlecombe and the Shakespearean actor David Troughton, father of Warwickshire captain Jim Troughton, been on a narrow boat holiday on the Avon in 2003. In the absence of their wives, it was effectively a water-borne pub crawl. At the Four Alls in Welford they bumped into Andy Lloyd, former Warwickshire and all too briefly England opener, who by that time was chairman of the county's Cricket Committee. 'Let's just say we had a little chat,' Paul confides in his compact office in the clubhouse. 'We'd staged

Lord's Taverners matches throughout the eighties and nineties as well as second-team games with high scores – six hundred runs in a day on one occasion. I just felt that the ground was in great shape to host county cricket. As it turned out, Lloyd agreed and so, eventually, did the Warwickshire committee.

Swan's Nest Lane is just across the river from the Royal Shakespeare Company's main house and the Swan Theatre. You can see their very different rooftops from the pavilion end. Rather more scenic is the view from what's known as the Swan's Nest end. The spire of Holy Trinity, the Bard's last resting place, protrudes elegantly between willow and poplar trees. Between them and the Avon is yet another line of cars. The ground is hemmed in by car parks on three sides and anyone who chooses to leave their vehicle within six-hitting distance does so at their windscreen's own risk. 'I've offered a bottle of champagne to anyone who can hit the notice in the public car park,' says David. The one listing the somewhat excessive charges that Stratford District Council evidently feels it can get away with? 'That's right. So far nobody's managed it.'

Troughton senior is a self-confessed cricket

nut who once played for a team of actors on Hampstead Heath known as the Weakenders (sic). He's a qualified umpire and used to score for Stratford during the nineties when he wasn't required onstage. 'I never did like matinees,' he confides. David's father, Patrick, played Dr Who in the long-running BBC TV series between 1966 and 1969, and his other two sons, Sam and Will ('Wigsy'), are both actors who have played cricket for Stratford. But Jim is the only male member of the family to have gone on to tread the turf (rather than the boards) professionally.

His return to the 'Nest' where he had scored so many runs as a youngster was not as happy as he might have hoped. At the end of what Halford describes in his book as a 'highly entertaining' first day against Lancashire, Warwickshire had reached 495 for 9, with Mark Waugh contributing 167 and Neil Carter thrashing 32 off 30 balls, including a six that almost sent a flutter through the nearby Butterfly Farm. Troughton, however, had been caught Law bowled Keedy for eight.

Meanwhile, his father had been overseeing litter collection. 'Charles Colvile [of Sky Sports] observed that I was the first Shakespearean actor he'd ever met emptying bins,' David recalls. Sky covered both matches at the Swan's Nest, much to the disgruntlement of the press and scorers who found themselves shunted off to cow corner. Their mood wasn't improved when the temperature dropped several degrees on the second day of the Lancashire game and twenty-eight overs were lost to rain, much of it coming into their tent horizontally on stiff breezes. But that was nothing compared with what happened next.

On the third day came a storm that made King Lear's experience on the blasted heath seem like a brief encounter with a light drizzle. Hailstones came down with considerable force. Halford records: 'They battered marquees and thundered into the pavilion roof. They pinged off visor of helmet, windscreen of Peugeot and beak of swan. Cricketers fled. Spectators scrambled for cover. Ground staff leapt into action. Within 10 minutes, incredibly, on June 20th for heaven's sake, the field was white.'

For chairman Paul the dream of hosting a

county match was turning into a nightmare. 'It was like an ice storm,' he reflects, shaking his head as if to dislodge a particularly painful memory. 'Luckily, our groundsman at the time, Geoff Calcutt, had brought in a lot of help for the week. So when the weather decided to throw everything at us, we had quite a few experts on hand.'

They managed to get play underway again by the end of the afternoon. By stumps Lancashire were 505 for 8 and the match was dead. It petered out into an inevitable draw on the Monday, by which time the crowd was considerably down on the three thousand or so who had turned up for the first day.

Stratford didn't have much luck in 2005 either, despite the presence of Shane Warne and Kevin Pietersen in the visiting Hampshire side that arrived at the end of May. Warne spent the warm-up period modelling suits for a photo-shoot, but still managed to turn in figures of 6 for 88, including an unplayable ball to Jim Troughton (22)

◀ **Left:** *The crowd at Stratford were far closer together than they are for county matches at Edgbaston.*

as Warwickshire responded to the visitors' 184 with 265. But it was the seamers who benefited most from overhead conditions. The ball began to swing around alarmingly during Hampshire's second innings. They were all out for 124, with Heath Streak and Dougie Brown sharing the spoils.

Nick Knight and Ian Westwood knocked off the runs required for a ten-wicket victory and a four-day match was over in two days – just what officials of Stratford CC could have done without. 'Friday was supposed to be the third day and we'd planned it to be the big corporate day for local businesses,' Paul recalls. 'At least the Warwickshire players came back and did some promotional work for us around the hospitality tents.' And did you make a loss? 'No, but we didn't make a profit either.' Even with Sky there? 'They pay the ECB [England and Wales Cricket Board], not us. Yes, I know; in football it's the clubs who get the money. At least our costs were underwritten by a company that Andy Lloyd had

some involvement with.'

The county's one-day match against Scotland, planned for the Sunday to complete a Stratford festival week, looked like being over in two hours. 'Warwickshire were seventeen for six at one point,' says Paul. 'But somehow they managed to get to a hundred and twenty something. Scotland won with a six off the last ball.'

Not into the river, we might add. It's too far away for the swans to be troubled by flying leather, but just close enough to flood the pitch at increasingly frequent intervals. Three times it happened in the winter of 2012–13. 'My beef is that they don't dredge the river,' says Paul. But, then, as Shakespeare put it, 'What fates impose that men must need abide, It boots not to resist both wind and tide.'

He wasn't writing about cricket for obvious reasons.

WORCESTERSHIRE

~

THE WAR MEMORIAL GROUND, AMBLECOTE, STOURBRIDGE

It was 29 July 1981: royal wedding day. The heir to the throne was preparing to marry Lady Diana Spencer and the nation was preparing for a knees-up after an eyes-down in front of the telly. Apart, that is, from the cricket lovers of Stourbridge and district. The nigh-on five thousand holiday crowd crammed into the War Memorial Ground were more interested in watching the first day of Worcestershire versus Northamptonshire. Tim Jones, now chairman of the Worcestershire CCC heritage group, was eighteen at the time and remembers squeezing into a temporary stand at the football club end of the ground. 'It's the only time I've not been able to get a scorecard in forty years of watching county cricket,' he recalls. 'They'd run out because there were so many there.'

Those who liked to see dashing batting would not be disappointed. The prolific New Zealander Glenn Turner was back at the Birmingham League club ground where he had tentatively played his way into English conditions and been given the bird for slow scoring on more than one occasion. This time he made up for it, racing to a century in ninety-eight minutes from ninety-five balls. He'd made over 120 by lunch and finished on 161 after being caught at mid-on from his first ill-timed shot. Inevitably it was dubbed a regal innings, 'fit for a Prince – and Princess'. And, typically, he followed up with another century in the second innings.

Turner is on a short but illustrious list of players, which includes Bradman, Grace, (Viv) Richards, Zaheer Abbas, Hobbs and Sutcliffe, to have achieved a century of centuries. In his book of the same name he recalls that day at Stourbridge, watching events at Westminster Abbey in one of the marquees right up to 10.45 a.m. He also reflects: 'When one plays on a ground not used to first-class cricket, one is doubtful of its lasting qualities and bats first [if one wins the toss, presumably]. I must say, though, that this wicket looked reasonable, apart from a couple of doubtful patches where it was very bare, and it lasted pretty well.'

Well enough for three declarations – two by Worcestershire and one by Northants – yet the match still ended in a draw with the visitors 199 for 8 at the end. 'There were quite a few draws here and there were some issues about the quality of the outfield,' says Stourbridge committee member Ken Workman. Sharing one side of it with the local football club is rarely a recipe for easy fielding in the deep, as anyone who played at Bramall Lane, Sheffield, or Park Avenue, Bradford, would testify.

That may be why, after venturing to Stourbridge for the first time in nineteen years, the county never returned for a first-class match – although they did come back for a one-day game against Leicestershire the following summer. Worcestershire had already given up on Tipton Road, Dudley, long before a 40-foot hole opened up in the outfield as a result of the limestone workings below. And they'd abandoned the evocatively named Chain Wire Ground at Stourport after just one game. Only Chester Road North in Kidderminster remained as a viable outground – to be reached for like an umbrella in case heavy rain caused the Severn to burst its banks and flood New Road at Worcester.

New Road was always an atmospheric ground, a personal favourite and one that inspired John Arlott to poetry about watching cricket through half-closed eyes while 'dozing in deck-chair's gentle curve'. That was in 1938. We can only imagine him looking down from his celestial deckchair in 2014 and shaking his head at the bustling new 120-bedroom Premier Inn with 'conferencing facilities' on the Severn side of the ground.

Amblecote, to the north of the River Stour and technically just over the county border into Staffordshire, seems comparatively quiet on a Saturday morning in March. The gateway to the ground is an imposing archway, sadly defaced across its lower quarters by adverts for local pizza and taxi companies. Heavy rain has given away to a light drizzle, but there are deep puddles on the walkway from the car park to the imposing pavilion. A sodden ball abandoned on the edge of the nets looks particularly forlorn and it's difficult to believe that the beginning of the new season is not much more than a month away. The poplar trees around the edge are still stark and wintry, unable to hide the ugly tower block protruding at what would be long-off for a right-hander taking guard at the pavilion end. At long on,

J.E. Timms and W.E. Brown returning to the Stourbridge pavilion in 1934 after Timms scored 213 for Northamptonshire. Doc Gibbons of Worcestershire is on the left.

by contrast, an unexpected patch of sun has just illuminated the Clent Hills like a promise of better tomorrows. That far side of the ground is known as the football end and the red-brick functionality of the football club's headquarters makes a marked contrast with the handsome church tower looming over the nearby cemetery and, indeed, that distinctive pavilion.

Opened in 1928 with money donated by local businessman Ernest Stevens and recently restored, it has a distinctive inter-war opulence about it – ornate windows, solid red-brick frontage and half-timbered gables. There's a clock tower topped by a weathercock on the roof where solar panelling has recently been installed. Candelabra dangle from mock beams inside and the panelled bar looks as though it should harbour men in demob suits smoking pipes under the fringed shades of standard lamps. Club chairman Harilal Patel shows me round

▼ **Below:** *The imposing gateway to Stourbridge's War Memorial Ground before it was covered in garish advertisements*

with justifiable pride, pointing out some of the pictures on the walls, including one of the senior Nawab of Pataudi who played here for Worcestershire in 1932 and twice in 1933. The thirties were heady days for Amblecote. The ground hosted annual festivals, fitting in two three-day county games in a week. We'll get back to that in a moment, but first let's make way for the force of nature that is David Banks.

The Stourbridge coach and former Worcestershire and Warwickshire batsman, a big man with a resounding Black Country voice, has just breezed into the pavilion. 'See that poplar tree,' he booms, pointing to the one at long-off. 'I hit a six over that once.' He was playing for Stourbridge against Wolverhampton at the time. 'The boundaries here,' he goes on, 'were not far short of New Road.' And the pitch? 'There was no comparison. The one at New Road was far better.' Which is another reason why Worcestershire, like most other counties, prefer to play at home rather than venturing to unpredictable outgrounds.

They came here for the first of sixty-one visits in 1905, well before it was rechristened the Memorial Ground, the pitch having been laid out as long ago as 1857. The match against Leicestershire was the county's first trip away from headquarters and they marked it with an innings victory. Fred Bowley hit 217 and Ted Arnold 134 in a total of 437. Arnold then followed up with match figures of 9 for 112 as the visitors were dismissed for 137 and 113.

But it was other visitors, ones from Kent, who put Amblecote, Stourbridge, into the record books four years later. Frank Woolley was joined by Arthur Fielder at the fall of the ninth wicket. Together they put on 235, a record tenth-wicket partnership in the County Championship. Woolley, one of the immortals, scored 185 and Fielder 112 not out, his only first-class century and the first ever by a number eleven at that level. Stourbridge had a thriving cut-glass industry and both batsmen were later presented with tumblers engraved with their face and name. In an interview with *The Cricketer Magazine*, Woolley revealed, shortly before he died in 1978, aged ninety-one, that he still had his tumbler at his home in Nova Scotia.

Ah, those glorious Edwardian summers of the Golden Age. Who could have known at the time of the coming carnage? Four of the players who graced that game, Colin Blythe and Kenneth Hutchings of Kent, William Burns and Harold Bache of Worcestershire, would perish on the Western Front.

Needless to say, the First World War was what the Memorial Ground was rechristened and re-gated to commemorate. As we've already noted, it would come into its own as the host of regular cricket festivals in the 1930s. By that time it had its own full-time groundsman. 'Arthur Fletcher his name was and he was so dedicated that he was on the verge of suicide when the county refused to supply him with some special fertiliser,' recalls former Worcestershire batsman and Stourbridge captain Norman Whiting. 'I can see his wife now with a rope round her waist pulling a mower across the square.'

Arthur obviously produced pitches that made things happen. One of Reg Perks's two first-class hat-tricks came in the game against Kent at Amblecote on 4 June 1931. Yorkshire rolled into town in 1936 and lost to Worcestershire for the first time since 1909 with Len Hutton bagging a rare 'pair'. He took revenge the following year by scoring 101 and helping Maurice Leyland (167) to add 233 for the third wicket. Yorkshire duly won by an innings with eighty-one runs to spare, but later that same June week the 'home' side went on to beat Glamorgan by nine wickets.

Norman first turned out for Stourbridge in 1938 when he was eighteen. He's now getting on for ninety-four, still playing golf and following the county around the country with his old pal Duncan Fearnley, who also wielded the willow for Worcs before becoming the most famous moulder of willow into bats in the country. These days Norman has a flat from which you can just about see New Road – which is ironic insofar as he insisted on travelling in from Stourbridge every day during his playing days. On the bus with him was another old pal, Don Kenyon, who would go on to play for England eleven times. 'We used to leave Stourbridge Bus Station at 8.30 and get here just in time to play,' Norman remembers. 'It took one and a half hours with a twenty-minute wait at Kidderminster.'

Both could have a lie-in when they played for the county back home at Amblecote during the 1950s when outground visits were becoming more sporadic. Its days as a regular first-class venue were almost numbered by 1960 when Kenyon hit a double century there against Glamorgan. 'But it still had the best pavilion on the circuit,' Norman maintains. 'New Road was tatty by comparison until they built the one named after Graeme Hick. By the sixties Stourbridge couldn't afford to keep a groundsman. I'd given up county cricket by then and I did the ground for five years after work [as a rep for a pharmaceutical company].'

Norman was well into his fifties when he took on the captaincy of Stourbridge second team. It was then that a young New Zealander came under his wing. Name of Turner. 'Glenn hardly hit the ball off the square, but he wanted to occupy the crease and learn. Yes, the crowd would sometimes give him the bird, but I picked the team and I could see he was going to be good.'

Turner would go on to show the cricket-lovers of Stourbridge and district just how good when he returned for Amblecote's last hurrah as a first-class ground one memorable day in 1981.

six County Championships in that decade were sealed here at St George's Road. Ray Illingworth, for instance, might have enjoyed taking fourteen wickets against Gloucestershire in 1967, topping off a two-day victory with 7 for 6 in the second innings.

Five years previously, a crowd of over 13,000 wedged in to see another Championship decider settled in the two dry days. This time the victims were Glamorgan, bowled out for 65 in their first innings. Don Wilson took the honours with 6 for 24.

Astonishingly, an even bigger crowd turned up here in 1996 and its make-up was rather different from the usual gathering of well-heeled Harrogate residents and farmers down from the Dales. Over 15,000 materialised in 1986 for a 'friendly' between India and Pakistan. 'Quite a few of them came in over the wall,' Bill recalls with a chuckle. 'At one point, the police were

threatening to call off the match because some of the Pakistan supporters were encroaching on the players' side of the boundary. There'd have been a riot if they had. So I found the ringleader and told him that if the ball hit one of them, it would be four runs to India. Within minutes, they'd all shot back behind the rope.'

Now you may be wondering why stars such as Sunil Gavaskar and Kapil Dev, Imran Khan and Wasim Akram had to find their way to Harrogate rather than Headingley. The answer is that the game was financed by a prosperous local Asian restaurateur.

Another local businessman, one Colin Clarke, helped to turn Yorkshire's annual visit from a three-day affair into a week-long festival. In 1974 he set up the Tilcon trophy, named after his construction company, to provide a competitive edge for one-day games between three counties, culminating in a final played at the weekend, The silver cup, about fifty times bigger than the Ashes urn, is still there on a shelf behind the pavilion bar. Needless to say, it's no longer played for. The Tilcon competition lasted for twenty years, after which it became, appropriately and all too briefly, the Costcutter Cup. Two years later, Harrogate was witnessing what turned out to be its last cricket festival.

The Tavern Bar, next door to the new pavilion, is now the Little Crickets nursery. 'My wife and I used to be really busy in there on festival days,' Robert Whiteley recalls. Too busy in 1979 to watch his brother, Peter, take 3 for 86 for Yorkshire in Somerset's second innings, accounting for Messrs Botham, Roebuck and Richards. Mind you, Viv had already scored 116 when he was finally caught Old bowled Whiteley. Five years earlier the great man had made 217 not out here – the first double-century in a county match at St George's Road since Percy Holmes's 277, also not out, in 1921.

It's all very difficult to imagine now. To the right of what used to be the Tavern is what was once the Mound stand. But any allusions to Lord's must have been ironic. Harrogate's Mound is really an elevated stretch of grass that housed at least half a dozen marquees at festival time. The rows of seats below them are now nothing more than stretches of concrete. Gone, too, is the old wooden stand that ran across the other side of the ground and most of the plastic seats that once swept around all the way from the Mound to the Tavern.

That Tavern Bar saw a fair amount of post-match carousing at festival time, particularly when Gloucestershire or Northamptonshire were the visitors. 'They were the kings of the social side,' Bill confides. He won't, however, disclose the name of the 'fast bowler of some repute' who 'disappeared under the [wicket] covers with a young lady late one night, much to the amusement of the few of us who were still there. His first ball the following morning was a long hop that was duly despatched to the boundary. The groundsman turned to me and said: "That's funny; he wasn't short of a length last night."'

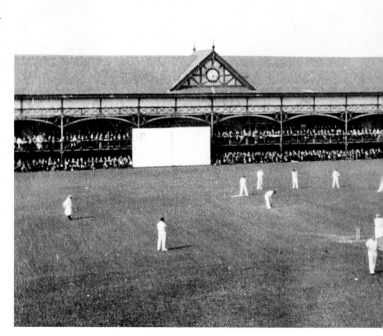

PARK AVENUE, BRADFORD

Brian Close was thought to be impervious to physical pain. Five years after his bruising confrontation with Wesley Hall in the 1963 Lord's Test match, he was leading Yorkshire to their third County Championship title on the trot – this time at the Circle in Hull where the former square is now inside the centre circle of Hull City Football Club's KC Stadium. Fielding at short leg, Close took a fearsome blow on the shin which rebounded into the gloves of Jimmy Binks. Despite blood seeping through his flannels, the skipper insisted on playing on until victory over Surrey was secured. Only then did he agree to go to hospital. 'And when I got back, the lads had drunk all the champagne,' he grumbled.

But Close would occasionally allow a chink of emotion to find a way through his craggy, armoured exterior, it seems. His return to Yorkshire with Somerset for a Sunday League game drew a crowd of around 15,000 to Park Avenue, Bradford, and every one of them stood to applaud him to the wicket. 'I think he was emotionally affected and he was out soon on,' says David Warner, president of the Cricket Writers' Club who had just started covering Yorkshire for the Bradford Telegraph and Argus around that time.

David is not alone in suggesting that Close, Illingworth, Hutton, Trueman and, particularly, Bob Appleyard liked playing at Bradford. 'It was more intimate than either Headingley or Bramall Lane,' he recalls. 'There were sizeable crowds and they were close to the pitch, banked up on steep sides. It was an amphitheatre that was known as the Bull Ring.'

For visiting teams it must have seemed quite intimidating, rather like the vibes coming from the Grinders' Stand on the Spion Kop at Bramall Lane where the men who ground steel for Sheffield cutlery gathered to pass sometimes voluble judgement. 'Park Avenue wasn't noted for giving stick so much as being a bastion of keen observation,' David goes on. 'But if the crowd had anything to say, there'd be plenty of it.'

From the 1880s onwards, Yorkshire visited Bradford several times a season, and that arrangement

▲ **Previous page:** *Play about to resume after an interval at Harrogate.*

▲ **Above:** *Crowds of 13,000 and more have wedged into the St George's Road ground.*

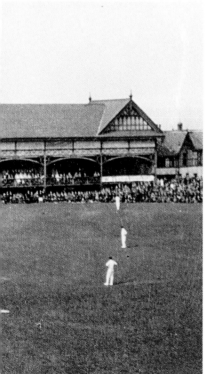

◀ **Left:** *Bradford Park Avenue drew sizeable crowds before and after the war.*

continued for much of the twentieth century. It was here that Percy Holmes made 275 against Warwickshire in 1928 and Emmott Robinson took a career best 9 for 36 in a Roses match in 1920. That was surpassed by Jim Laker thirty years later. In the 'Test Trial' of 1950 he took 8 for 2 in 14 overs as 'The Rest' were skittled for 27. The Rest included Peter May, his future captain of England as well as Surrey.

By the 1990s, however, Park Avenue was restricted to one first-class match a season. One-day games had ceased in the mid-eighties, by which time the imposing Victorian pavilion, like the nearby football stand, had been dismantled for safety reasons. But before the county pulled up the Headingley drawbridge almost completely, Bradford was granted a one-day as well as a four-day game against Leicestershire, in June 1996.

In the Championship match, the visitors had the effrontery to compile 681 for 7, with Vince Wells and James Whitaker scoring double centuries. Leicestershire romped home by an innings. But at least the locals had something to cheer in the one-dayer, which Yorkshire won by 38 runs.

Bradford pavilion with large
crowds gathered.

By that time, Park Avenue was feeling its age. These days it's looking its age, too, plagued by vandalism and requiring considerable investment. Bradford Park Avenue cricket and football clubs long ago departed for pastures new and even the local university side pulled out in 2004 after having to clear the outfield of syringes before play could commence. It's still used by a club called Wibsey Park Chapel, which plays in the Towergate Halifax Cricket League. But to Bradfordians and many more Tykes of a certain age it will always be remembered as the Bull Ring that encompassed the heart and soul of Yorkshire cricket.

ACKLAM PARK, MIDDLESBROUGH

Fred Trueman was never asked to play in a Test match at Chester-le-Street in May. Just as well, perhaps. He once described Acklam Park, Middlesbrough (forty miles south of Durham's headquarters), as the furthest north a cricketer could be asked to go without entering the Arctic Circle.

Well, the breeze off the River Tees could make it a bit parky at times, though fast bowlers seem to have worked up a fair head of steam on what was considered the quickest wicket in Yorkshire at one time. Back in 1963, Charlie Griffith hit Doug Padgett and Jackie Hampshire on the head while playing for the West Indies against a Yorkshire side that still went on to win by 111 runs, with Fred taking five wickets in each innings.

Two years later, the 'home' side suffered the ignominy of being bowled out for 23 by Hampshire in their second innings, Butch White finishing with figures of 6 for 10. But Fred would no doubt have preferred to remember the first innings in which he scored a characteristically belligerent 55, including 26 off one over from Derek Shackleton.

Geoffrey Boycott (out for nought and five against Hants) would prefer to remember making his 150th hundred here in 1986 against Leicestershire, putting him one ahead of Herbert Sutcliffe as Yorkshire's leading century-maker. And Chris Old, Middlesbrough-born and bred, no doubt recalls delighting his home crowd by taking 7 for 20 in 1969 as Gloucestershire were dismissed for 41 in their first innings.

Although Acklam Park hosted first-class cricket only from 1956 to 1996, another local lad, the author Harry Pearson, remembers the ground 'having a feel of permanence about it'. Not much temporary seating had to be brought in for county games because there were terraces of wooden benches. They stretched a fair way around the perimeter and helped to accommodate a crowd of over 13,000 for a Championship match against Warwickshire in 1967. They were backless benches that Jim Kilburn of the Yorkshire Post felt became 'a trial in a full day's watching'. But, then, Kilburn was a great fan of the

◀ **Opposite top:** *Chris Old back on his home-town ground.*

◀ **Left:** *Former Middlesbrough manager Jack Charlton tries his hand at another sport.*

◀ **Bottom left:** *Bramall Lane, the grittiest ground in Yorkshire.*

Scarborough festival (see page 186) and much of the seating there is similarly spartan. 'Hard-core Yorkshiremen wouldn't want to spend much money on seat backs,' says Harry, the author of *Slipless in Settle*, the affectionate yet irreverent guide to northern club cricket.

The compact pavilion at Acklam Park had to be enhanced by marquees when the county came to town. And in the winter months it was given over to the men who played on the adjoining rugby union pitch. Well, at least it made a change from sharing a ground with association football, as at Bramall Lane and Bradford Park Avenue, and rugby league, as at Fartown, Huddersfield. It was at Fartown that Boycott famously lost his contact lens during a Sunday League game in 1974, shortly after going wild and hitting a six out of the ground. Hundreds of spectators joined the fruitless search for the lens.

After that incident, Boycott always carried a spare pair. Otherwise he might never have reached that 150th hundred on a memorable day in Middlesbrough.

NORTH MARINE ROAD, SCARBOROUGH

It's 28 August 2013 and, although the football season has been underway for what seems like weeks, the winter of our discontent is some way off and it's still glorious summer by this sun of Yorkshire.

The Scarborough Cricket Festival is already underway and, according to local radio, Durham have lost early wickets with Ryan Sidebottom doing the damage and closing in on his 600th first-class wicket. This is a match between the top two teams that could go a long way to deciding the County Championship. Appropriately enough, the biggest crowd of the season has turned up. One of these days I might be joining them, I reflect, as my car inches forward in a huge traffic jam on the A64 somewhere near York.

Scarborough is not a lost festival, of course. Anything but. After recent ground improvements, largely paid for by sponsorship from Tesco and its suppliers, Yorkshire CCC has confirmed its status as the only 'home' ground that will see them make annual forays from Headingley until at least 2020. This in by far the largest English county that once had outgrounds from Sheffield to Middlesbrough, Bradford to Hull, and several places in between.

Be that as it may, Scarborough's survival and revival is something to celebrate in a book tinged with regret at the loss of so many festival venues in England and Wales.

By the time I'm finally walking towards the ground from the park-and-ride stop, every other person seems to be tucking into fish and chips. Well, this is a seaside town and the success of the festival has been built on staging it to take place during the school holidays when, as Scarborough CC chairman Bill Mustoe tells me, the population increases from 60,000 to 'a quarter of a million plus'.

Over five and a half thousand of them have found their way into this historic cricket ground today and similar numbers will turn up on the three remaining days. 'It will go a long way to helping us

recover from the £80,000 loss that we made in 2012 when the weather was terrible,' says Bill.

Yorkshire will take a percentage of the profits and the size of this year's crowds will make that a more than satisfactory return. Unlike most festival grounds, the county doesn't have to spend money on importing temporary seating. Here is an already established arena – an intimate arena, if that doesn't sound too contradictory. There's supposed to be room for another nigh-on four thousand spectators, yet there doesn't seem to be too much spare space on rows of wooden benches descending towards the boundary. Even here on the back row, with North Marine Road and the sea just behind us, you feel close to the action.

Durham have made a good recovery, thanks to spirited resistance from Mark Stoneman and Ben Stokes, both of whom will go on to make centuries. Entertaining cricket, then, in a setting very different from Cheltenham or Chesterfield. On the other side of the ground, seagulls are swooping over slate roofs and distant hills loom over flapping flags. Opposite the red-brick pavilion is the peeling stucco of four-storey boarding houses that face on to Trafalgar Square. Their windows have been the target of big-hitting batsmen from the Victorian heyday of the festival's founder, C.I. 'Buns' Thornton, onwards. To our right, guests are sitting on the balcony of the Boundary Hotel like theatregoers who have booked a box.

It feels good to be here in the clear sea air once I've seen off a belated lunch – a polystyrene plate of chips washed down with a pint of Boddington's. Yes, Boddington's, once as much a part of Manchester as Tetley's was of Leeds. These days they're both brewed elsewhere, which makes it less of a cross-Pennine issue than it would have been at one time.

My beer has been bought by Duncan Hamilton, the biographer of Harold Larwood and author of *A Last English Summer,* which managed to make me nostalgic for Scarborough while I read it lying on a beach in the South of France. North

Scarborough Festival time: one of the fixed points of the cricketing calendar.

Marine Road is very special to Duncan, as it was for another former *Yorkshire Post* man from a different generation. 'Whenever a pilgrimage through the cricketer's England may begin,' wrote J.M. [Jim] Kilburn, 'it must surely end, if the traveller has any sense of the appropriate, at Scarborough in Festival time . . . To have made one visit is almost certain infection for the desire to return. Two visits make it virtually the establishment of a habit . . .'

Well, Duncan has certainly caught the habit. He's a regular, and not just for the first day. Been here on days when the wind has whipped in from the North Sea and both Inzamam-ul-Haq and Michael Vaughan took to the field in white woolly hats; and he's been here when a sea fret spread across the outfield 'like a muslin veil' and stopped play against Warwickshire. That was in 2007. Three years before, he saw Ricky Ponting make a classical century for Somerset on his Championship debut for Somerset.

'Ponting looked capable,' he wrote, 'of outstripping some of the highest scores on the ground: Hobbs's unbeaten 266 for the Players against the Gentlemen in 1928, Hutton's unbeaten 266 for the Players against the Gentlemen in 1928, Hutton's unbeaten 241 in the same fixture twenty-five years later or the 202 Herbert Sutcliffe took off Middlesex in 1936. Even the most partisan Yorkshireman put aside county loyalty, grateful instead just to watch Ponting bat. And then, for a microsecond, Ponting lost his focus and his wicket . . . Like a mourner unwilling to leave a graveside, Ponting didn't move at first. When he did so, he took the pavilion steps two at a time, stomped into the dressing rooms, threw his bat against the wall and simultaneously uttered a long, loud oath which could be heard throughout the pavilion.'

During the tea interval, I belatedly discover the seafood stall, only to discover that they've sold out of crab sandwiches. Crayfish tails don't sound quite so appealing in this setting, so I join the crowds strolling out on to the flat and springy outfield where impromptu matches with tennis balls are quickly underway. One elderly lady has strolled right across the wicket, much to the annoyance of a security guard who calls after her, to no avail. 'You could do with a lasso sometimes,' he mutters. Well, at least

she's not wearing heels.

Signing autographs on the boundary is Dickie Bird who no doubt has plenty of Scarborough memories, some fond, like the time he hit Frank Tyson for two successive fours; some not so fond, like being taken to hospital after Tyson responded with a bouncer, strode down the pitch and said: 'Try and hit that one for four, you bastard.'

After play resumes, there's a bit of a lull in the Tesco-sponsored tea bar. One of the many women in pinnies behind the counter seems only too glad to have someone to serve. I'm taking my plastic cup back to my seat to watch Paul Collingwood take over from where Stoneman and Stokes have left off. But I can't help noting another elderly lady, sitting under a cartoon of Jimmy Binks and setting about a slice of chocolate cake, dextrously wielding a white plastic spoon as though it were a silver pastry fork.

By the end of the day, Durham have reached 406 for 6. Not bad for a side that was 10 for 3 at one point. A great day's entertainment, for sure, and proof that cricket festivals staging four-day games can thrive and make money.

Increasing numbers of gulls are now swooping over the outfield, and I can almost detect an autumnal nip in the air. A memorable summer is coming to a close. England have retained the Ashes and I've travelled far and wide, talking to cricket lovers with treasured memories of the days when the counties travelled widely, too.

Duncan will be coming back to North Marine Drive again tomorrow. Me? I'm heading south in the fond hope that the A64 might be a little less congested by now.

On the way back to the park-and-ride depot, I find myself recalling the places I've been and the grounds that I've seen. Even on rainy days, the magisterial settings of Abergavenny and Buxton had evoked the ghosts of memorable days in the sun (and the snow in Buxton's case). Bournemouth had looked timelessly sedate, even in the chill of the early season. Bath's Recreation Ground had been bathed in hot July sun, the outfield parched and the pavilion in need of repair. The elegant buildings and surrounding hills made it one of the most scenic places to watch cricket, as long as you had your back to the hideous sports and leisure centre.

But the Recreation Ground is exactly that: a recreation ground that doesn't even host a club cricket. Perhaps only a county cricket club would make the effort to transform a public park, over seventy miles from its headquarters in Taunton, into a venue for watching professional sport. And Somerset did it almost every

year for well over a century. Everything had to be brought in, including seating and, for much of the twentieth century at least, PA systems, running water and electricity. This for a game that is so dependent on good weather in a country that can never guarantee it.

The decline of the cricket festival, in Somerset and elsewhere, is hardly surprising for reasons that have been discussed elsewhere in this book. But some long-running festivals are defying the odds. Scarborough is one, Cheltenham another. Not only are they providing rich entertainment for lovers of the four-day game; they're also making money for their respective counties. That's the best hope of survival for festivals anywhere. As the sun begins to set on what has been a glorious summer and a memorable season, that in turn provides a ray of hope for those of us who never want to see an endangered species become extinct.

An appealing venue in more ways than one.

BIBLIOGRAPHY

Arlott, John (editor), *My Favourite Cricket Stories*, Peerage Books (1974)

Bailey, Trevor, *Wickets, Catches and the Odd Run*, Willow Books Collins (1986)

Chalke, Stephen, *The Way It Was: Glimpses of English cricket's past*, Fairfield Books, and *Runs in the Memory: County Cricket in the 1950s* (2008) and *Runs In The Memory: County Cricket in the 1950s* (1997)

Engel, Matthew (editor): *The Guardian Book of Cricket*, Pavilion (1986)

Engel, Matthew, and Radd, Andrew, *The History of Northamptonshire County Cricket Club*, Christopher Helm, London (1993)

Foot, David, *Harold Gimblett: Tormented Genius of Cricket*, Heinemann (2003)

Halford, Brian, *The Year of the Bear: The story of Warwickshire's 2004 Championship Triumph*, Parrs Wood Press (2005)

Hamilton, Duncan, *A Last English Summer*, Quercus (2010)

Hughes, Simon, *A Lot of Hard Yakka: Triumph and Torment: a County Cricketer's Life*, Headline (1997)

Pearson, Harry, *Slipless in Settle*, Littlebrown (2010)

Plumptre, George, *Homes of Cricket: The First-Class Grounds of England and Wales*, MacDonald Queen Anne Press (1988)

Powell, William, *Cricket Grounds of Surrey*, ACS Publications (2001)

Smith, Martin (editor), *The Promise of Endless Summer: Cricket Lives from the* Daily Telegraph, Aurum Press (2013)

PICTURE CREDITS